GEORGE MacBEATH

New Brunswick's Old Government House

A Pictorial History

Dear Inspector Reverge,

A token of my appreciation for your distinguished and devoted service as my Aide-de-Camp,

Marilyn Trenholme Counsell
Lieutenant Governor N.B.

New Ireland Press

Copyright © George MacBeath 1995

New Ireland Press
217 Aberdeen Street
Fredericton, New Brunswick
E3B 1R6

Typesetting by Cummings Imagesetting, Fredericton, New Brunswick.
Book and cover design by Sheena Dougan

We gratefully acknowledge the assistance of the Canada Council and the New Brunswick Department of Municipalities, Culture and Housing.

Canadian Cataloguing in Publication Data

    MacBeath, George, 1924-

    New Brunswick's Old Government House

    Includes bibliographical references.
    ISBN 0-920483-88-7

1. Government House (Fredericton, N.B.) 2. Historic buildings -- New Brunswick -- Fredericton.
3. Fredericton (N.B.) -- Buildings, structures, etc.
I. Title. II. Title: Old Government House.

FC2496.8.G68M34 1994   971.5'515   C94-950272-3
F1044.5.F8M34 1994

Cover illustration: *Government House, Fredericton.*
Hand-coloured lithograph from a drawing made in 1832 by Edward Thomas Coke.

*This book is dedicated to Old Government House.
May its future prosper!*

Contents

Acknowledgements vii

Foreword ix

By Way of Introduction xi

One The Birth of a Province 15

Two A Chivalrous Era 19

Three A Colonial Social Centre 29

Four Changing Times 37

Five Government House and Confederation 44

Six From Rebirth to Twilight Years 50

Seven Neglect, Closing and Thereafter 57

Postscript 64

Appendix 67

References 73

Acknowledgements

Indebtedness to the many writers, past and present, who provided facts and insights which made this volume possible, is gratefully noted. Special thanks go to the obliging Legislative Library staff members, as well as those of the Provincial Archives, the New Brunswick Museum, the Beaverbrook Art Gallery, the National Archives, the Royal Ontario Museum and the York-Sunbury Historical Museum. There was a special pleasure, too, in being able to draw upon the holdings of the Government House Collection.

To be cited for grateful thanks is Professor Tim Dilworth, who unselfishly shared his impressive knowledge of New Brunswick cabinet-makers. It was fortunate as well to be able to draw upon the advice and expertise of the late Dr. R.H. Hubbard, author of *Ample Mansions*; Marie Elwood, History Curator Emeritus with the Nova Scotia Museum; Peter Winkworth of London, Honorary Curator of the McCord Museum; and A.J.H. Richardson, Architectural Historian and former Secretary of the Historic Sites and Monuments Board of Canada.

Her Honour Dr. Margaret McCain graciously agreed to supply the foreword to this volume, and that important contribution is acknowledged with sincere thanks.

I was very fortunate to have Emelie Hubert Seheult as my assistant for three years, when the research for this publication was first undertaken. More recently she has made many helpful suggestions, and she assisted with the locating of the pictorial material so essential to this volume.

Lastly, indebtedness to my wife, Dr. Marie MacBeath, needs to be expressed. Her interest, effective encouragement, knowing eye and word processing skill made the manuscript possible during the many steps in its preparation.

Foreword

History and traditions define who we are and what we are as a people. Particularly in times of uncertainty and difficulty our roots provide us with the stability to adapt to the forces of change. The second half of the 20th century has been an era of unprecedented social and political change. Concurrently, throughout the world we have witnessed a powerful awakening of interest in people's cultural heritage.

In New Brunswick, nestled in quiet dignity along the banks of the St. John River, is one of North America's finest examples of Regency architecture. It sits as a living symbol of a proud, enduring people. Built to replace the viceregal residence, which had been destroyed by fire in 1825, it weaves together the threads of New Brunswick's rich history and heritage. It was built by the English colonial government of the day on land that once was the site of an Acadian village, and beside an ancient Maliseet burying ground.

Proudly defying the ravages of time, its firm foundation speaks to New Brunswick people of themselves. It testifies to a proud, hardy people living together in a peaceful land whose parts have been cemented together into a rich and beautiful symmetry.

Official flag of Her Honour, the Lieutenant Governor. It is described as being of royal blue, with a shield containing the arms of the province, within a circlet of maple leaves representing the ten provinces. The surmounting Crown indicates that she is the Sovereign's representative in New Brunswick.

Present-day privy seal of New Brunswick's Lieutenant Governor.

Old Government House: a pictorial history

A modern-day view of Old Government House. The structure is still impressive to behold, having worn its years well. The restoration of this "grand old home" as the viceregal residence is soon to begin.

New Brunswick Photographic Services

The Lieutenant Governor, through the constitutional head of a provincial government, is, in the modern context, a servant of the people.

A viceregal residence also belongs to the people and its primary function must be to serve them. The residence should therefore reflect the history and culture of the people in that particular province or country.

Some Canadian provinces have no viceregal residence, some have purchased residences, while others built residences when they became a province or joined Confederation. Our first viceregal residence was built in 1787 when the colony of Nova Scotia divided into two parts, creating the new province we now know as New Brunswick. The present building, which replaced the original, pre-dates Confederation by close to forty years. For the past one hundred years it has not been used as a viceregal residence. Nevertheless, it has remained an enduring symbol of our heritage and traditions. It has a magnetic pull on the hearts and souls of the New Brunswick people and continues to cry out to us for renewed life. Happily that cry has now been heard.

I highly commend Dr. George MacBeath for his commitment and dedication to New Brunswick history and, in particular, the history of this magnificent building. Through his efforts in reviving Old Government House he has reactivated pride in our provincial heritage.

The Honourable Margaret Norrie McCain
Lieutenant Governor
Province of New Brunswick

By Way of Introduction

And Nobleness walks in our ways again; And we have come into our heritage.
— Rupert Brooke

Old Government House is one of those majestic buildings which stands on land remarkably rich in historical associations. That property is the flat river terrace beside the St. John River which served Native peoples as a seasonal camp for many thousands of years both in pre-contact and historic times. Acadians made homes for themselves on the site as early as 1713, and by 1733 their settlement—Sainte-Anne by name—was the dominant francophone community on the river. During the 1755 Expulsion of the Acadians from Grand Pré, Sainte-Anne became a gathering place for refugee families, some remaining, others moving to more secure locations. In 1759, New England rangers destroyed the settlement, burning 142 buildings, including the chapel and the priest's residence.

Following the destruction of the Acadian village, the firm of Simonds, Hazen and White established a major trading facility at Sainte-Anne. The province of Nova Scotia, which at that time included present-day New Brunswick, appointed Benjamin Atherton, the trading firm's agent, Clerk of the Peace and Registrar of Sunbury County, thereby establishing a governmental and administrative presence on the St. John River.

In 1787, Atherton sold his parcel of land to Thomas Carleton, New Brunswick's first governor. There it was that the Governor built a home for his wife and himself, calling it Mansion House. Since he had chosen Sainte-Anne to be the

The quality of the new viceregal building attracted international attention. An example is this German engraving of the newly erected gubernatorial edifice at Fredericton. It is a rather poor print, obviously based on the drawing by the "anonymous lady" in Lieutenant-Colonel Joseph Bouchette's *The British Dominions in North America*.

New Brunswick Government House Collection

new province's capital, his new abode became the viceregal residence. Subsequently it was purchased by the New Brunswick government and filled the role of official residence until it was destroyed by fire in 1825.

That first gubernatorial dwelling was replaced by the stately stone mansion which is the subject of this book. That noble structure was inspired by one of our ablest lieutenant governors, Sir Howard Douglas, designed by J.E. Woolford of Fredericton, and constructed under the supervision of Jedediah Slason to be the residence and office of the Crown's representative in New Brunswick. Professor W.S. MacNutt, speaking at the national historic sites ceremonies in 1962, made a statement well worth repeating:

> One of the truly notable things that today gives us reason for meditation is that the province was able, at a time when its population was less than 150,000, to raise and sustain this magnificent residence for the popular lieutenant-governor, Sir Howard Douglas. The revenues that paid for it were entirely provincial in origin.

Government House was to have a long and distinguished place in the life of New Brunswick. However, in 1893 it ceased to be used as the viceregal residence when the Legislative Assembly refused to make any further appropriations for its upkeep. Four years later its contents were dispersed by public auction and the building was officially closed as Government House.

After that date, it was at times vacant, but for periods it was used for a number of other purposes. During the First World War, Old Government House was taken over by the military, and in the last years of that conflict changes were made to adapt the building for use as a rehabilitation centre. Most striking of those alterations was the replacing of the third-storey windows with dormers, to provide increased space to better accommodate 450 wounded soldiers.

By a 1921 act of the provincial Legislative Assembly, sale of Old Government House to the federal government was authorized. Soon after, New Brunswick accepted a price of $50,000 for the building and its extensive grounds. Sadly, after serving for many years as RCMP "J" Division Headquarters the building is once again vacant.

The story of the governors and viceregal residences in the territory we today call New Brunswick remains largely to be told, and thereby to enrich the heritage we enjoy as New Brunswickers. Here, in our part of the New World, that story stretches back in time to the year 1604. That was when Pierre du Gua, Sieur de Monts, arrived as commissioned representative of the King of France, with instructions "to maintain, keep, and preserve the said regions under our power and authority."

In his book *Ample Mansions*, R.H. Hubbard has observed:

> By one of history's minor quirks the site of the first dwelling of a royal representative in French Canada is now in the United States. The tiny Ile Sainte-Croix, now called Dochet Island, lies in the middle of the St. Croix River, which bounds the province of New Brunswick on the west.

Dochet Island and the Sieur de Monts were at the beginning. Governor de Monts was to be followed by a series of distinguished individuals important to our rich history. Those successive governors who came after were French, British, even Dutch, and then Canadian, as the years passed and the panorama unfolded.

No less a personage than Samuel de Champlain made a drawing of the official residence of the Sieur de Monts on Dochet Island. The dwelling had been constructed of "fair sawn lumber" which had been brought from France.

The sketch, entitled "logis du Sieur de Mons," found its way into the pages of *Les Voyages de Samuel de Champlain*, published in 1613. It forms but a part of a larger view of the entire Ile Ste. Croix settlement.

Webster Canadiana Collection, New Brunswick Museum

By Way of Introduction

Left: Regrettably, no authentic picture of the Sieur de Monts exists. However, there is this imaginary portrait, to be found in the collections of the Massachusetts Archives.

Below: The de Monts coat of arms, a drawing with designs symbolic of his family history, is impressively described as being "d'azur, a trois monts d'or, sur montes d'un lambal ande d'or et sable de huit pieces."

Webster Canadiana Collection, New Brunswick Museum

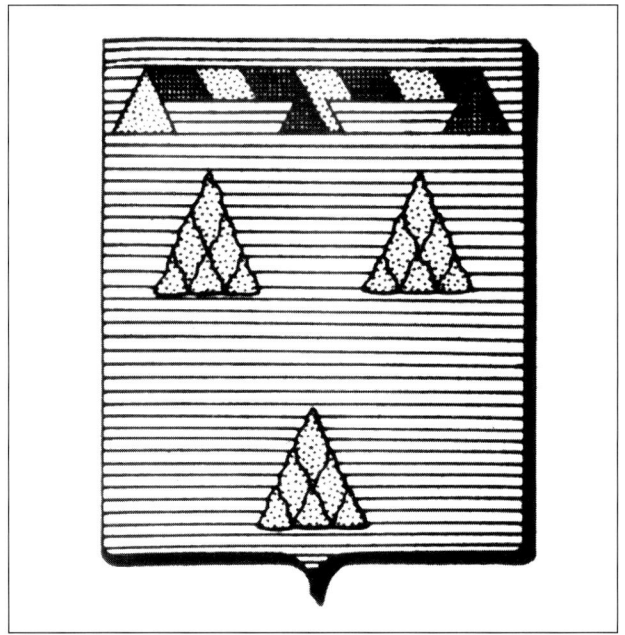

Today the province's representative of the Crown is the Lieutenant Governor, whose official residence is customarily referred to as Government House. No attempt has been made in this historical account to mention each and every Lieutenant Governor who has served New Brunswick. Instead, an official list of Their Excellencies is to be found as an appendix to this volume.

In preparing this work, I have filled many gaps in my own knowledge, and I hope I have provided both insights and enjoyment to readers of this volume. Its focus has been placed on Old Government House and its history. This study reveals something of the building's background, and of its construction, its distinctiveness and its place in our history, together with glimpses of its occupants and some of the memorable events with which it is associated. By way of clarification, I should note that the term "Old Government House" seems to have come into use when the building no longer served as the viceregal residence.

A fitting paragraph to this preface is supplied by historian Stewart MacNutt, during a lecture he gave in 1962:

> If we Canadians let our memories die there is no hope that our still immature nationality can become fully grown. Around Government House there is a great galaxy of memories that will become, we must hope, more vivid and meaningful with the passing of the years.

Old Government House: a pictorial history provides an overview, a popular account focused primarily on the building itself. Yet it does not ignore the occupants and visitors, their social activity and the many events of note associated with that handsome old structure. Many of its attractions are portrayed, as are its connections with the early governors of New Brunswick. Perhaps most important of all, it reveals something of the part that gubernatorial residence played in our province's growth and development.

George MacBeath, Fredericton, N.B.

One

The Birth of a Province

Following the Revolutionary War, those Americans who had remained loyal to the British Crown were obliged to leave their homes and country. Many of them sought a new life to the north of the new United States of America. Their coming brought into being in 1784 another province within British North America: New Brunswick.

Named by King George III to be its first governor was Thomas Carleton, a military officer who had served in the recent conflict. Carleton was a controversial individual: arrogant, able, snobbish and forceful are words that readily come to mind in describing his character. Yet he is the person who deserves the prime credit for taking the largely unsettled northern half of Nova Scotia and making it into a functioning, believable new colony. His effort was impressive and his accomplishments many. He was in command and he let everyone know it as he achieved his goals for the infant province.

A large and impressive oil on canvas portrait of King George III, by Sir Joshua Reynolds. His Majesty had already reigned twenty-four years when he created the province of New Brunswick, naming it after his family's ancestral seat in Germany. Now the painting is to be found at the Legislative Assembly Building, in the Assembly Chamber. It is a striking presence there, strategically located as it is to the side of the Throne, and providing a full measure of regal presence.

Speaker of the Legislative Assembly

Old Government House: a pictorial history

An oil on ivory miniature portrait of General Thomas Carleton, New Brunswick's Governor from the province's formation in 1784 until his death in 1817. It is believed to be the work of English artist Sampson Towgood Roche, and to date from about 1795.
Beaverbrook Art Gallery

As colonial administrator, Carleton was quick to address a host of challenges in achieving a well-governed colony. He saw to the needs of the recently arrived Loyalists, toured New Brunswick extensively, selected its capital, formed a government, arranged for the first elections and set up the province's defences.

Having made his choice as the site of the capital of New Brunswick, Carlton wrote from Saint John, then called Parr Town, to the Home Office directed by Lord Sydney.

PARR TOWN, NEW BRUNSWICK,
25th of April, 1785.

MY LORD,
I have the honor to inform Your Lordship that having in the course of last winter, visited the principal Settlements forming on St. John's River, I have fixed on St. Ann's Point, about Seventy-five miles from the mouth of the River, as a Station well situated for the future Seat of the Provincial Government. It has the advantage of being nearly in the centre of the Province, and within a few miles of that part beyond which the River ceases to be navigable for Vessels of any considerable size. Here the foundations are preparing for the Metropolis of New Brunswick, to which, as a mark of respect to His Royal Highness the Duke of York, I have given the name of Frederickstown, which I hope may meet with His Majesty's Approbation.
I have the Honor to be, My Lord
Your Lordship's
Most obedient and humble Servant
THOs. CARLETON

RIGHT Honb. LORD SYDNEY

In his beautiful and lovingly written chapter on New Brunswick in *Picturesque Canada*, Sir Charles G.D. Roberts explains the choice of Fredericton—then called Sainte Anne—to be the capital city:

> About four miles long and a mile in breadth, watered by small brooks, wooded with elms of fairest proportion, clear of underbrush as a well-kept park, and carpeted waist-deep with luxurious grasses, it was certainly a tempting spot upon which to found a city. Not for the loveliness of the spot, however, was it chosen to hold the capital of the infant Province; strategical considerations moved the soul of Sir Thomas.... Fredericton owed its birth, and for long its existence, to the military spirit engendered by the War of Independence. St. John was open to attacks from hostile New England; and, moreover, it had speedily become obvious that its spirit would be aggressively commercial. It is hard to say which of these was in the eyes of Sir Thomas the greater evil. He saw that St. Anne's Point was a fair spot, easy of settlement, admirably adapted for defense, almost inaccessible by land, and not easily accessible by water save for ships of light draught. Against these, also, a few cannon on the heights below the town, at Simonds Creek, would be an adequate protection. From the military point of view, then, Sir Thomas had every reason to be satisfied with Fredericton.

The first official seal of New Brunswic granted in 1785. Placed on documer signed by the Lieutenant Governor, it was composed of paper-covered wax. The face shown here is of a ship going up a river with pine trees crowding the banks. The Latin motto displayed is "Spem Reduxit" ("Hope Restored"), while around the margin is inscribed "Sigill. Provincae. Nov. Bruns." The other face of the seal has the British coat of arms, together with th(inscription "Georgius Tertium Dei Gr Brittaniarum Rex Defensor."

P.A.N.B.
(P110-2)

The Birth of a Province

It was Governor Carleton's firm intention "to hold the Reins of Government with a straight hand, and to punish the refractory with firmness." And as his January 1786 observations also noted, "put the finishing hand to the arduous task of organizing the Province." Edward Winslow, a leading New Brunswicker of the day, affirmed that Carleton was "a man whose dignified and correct conduct discountenanced vice and rendered morality fashionable."

In 1787 Governor Carleton "had caused to be built" at his own expense New Brunswick's first Government House. It was situated at the western outskirts of town, on the beautiful site where today we find its replacement, Old Government House. Mansion House, as it was called, was a pleasing two and one-half storey wooden building, with a truncated gable roof and a small wing at either end. Its "charming" gardens came to be the showplace of Fredericton, while the viceregal residence itself proved to be the large, comfortable, hospitable structure he and his lady wanted for their domain beside the majestic St. John. There he dwelled, met with his governing council, and entertained the privileged, monarchists through and through, in a world of long ago. Describing its public room in a 1901 talk before the Imperial Order of the Daughters of the Empire, Sarah H. McKee said:

> At this time the Government House drawing room was indeed an apartment of costly elegance. Richly coloured and gilded furniture were arranged in stately profusion; rare paintings adorned the frescoed walls; priceless cabinets, vases and statuary were grouped with artistic hand; Turkey carpets of the most brilliant hues covered the floors, while the light radiating from the massive chandelier made the scene one of surpassing grandeur.

Above: An appealing view of New Brunswick's first Government House. Besides the house, of special note are the sentry box and the sundial. The building was impressively sited adjacent to the St. John River. Wash drawing, likely by J.E. Woolford.

Royal Ontario Museum

Below: This wood engraving of Mansion House, residence of General Thomas Carleton, is credited to C.H. Flewwelling and possibly done from a drawing by J.E. Woolford.

From J.W. Lawrence's Footprints
P.A.N.B.
(P4-3-92)

Old Government House: a pictorial history

After Governor Carleton left for England, General Sir Martin Hunter was one of several officers appointed for various periods to act in his absence. He was given the title of "Administrator" and moved into Mansion House. Our best descriptions of that structure are provided by his wife, Lady Hunter. She wrote letters home, and impressive they are. Writing on May 24, 1808, she enthused:

> The house is large and commodious, with one most magnificent room. The situation the finest in the world, I do think, as to the picturesque and romantic, and far beyond any description of mine. We have a charming garden in the highest imaginable order, with a terrace to the river. . . . The Duke of Kent [father of Queen Victoria] when here told Governor Carleton he thought the view from the garden terrace exceeded that of Windsor.

The province purchased Mansion House in 1816, to have it continue as the official governor's residence to house the monarch's representatives, their families and household. By 1825, however, its last occupant, Sir Howard Douglas, claimed it was in disrepair and generally shabby. Not long after the building caught fire and was destroyed.

Within a very few years of worsening economic times for New Brunswick, mainly due to a slump in the timber trade, the elected Assembly began questioning the authority the vigorous Governor was exercising, as well as some of the actions he had taken. A prickly, ever elitist Carleton found this challenge to his authority hard to cope with. That was the principal reason for his leaving the province in 1803, to return to England. There he remained, still as Lieutenant Governor, working on behalf of New Brunswick until his death in 1817.

The government of New Brunswick placed a bronze plaque in the Church of St. Swithin's in England, to commemorate his contribution to the province. It reads: "Beneath this church lies the body of General Thomas Carleton, Governor of the Province of New Brunswick from its foundation in 1784 until his death in 1817. Erected by the Legislature of New Brunswick."

As his biographer, W.G. Godfrey, has observed, "Perhaps among the most attractive qualities of the crusty old soldier were his bluntly straightforward approach when aroused and the honest evaluation of both his own and New Brunswick's problems." So passed a memorable period in the province's beginnings.

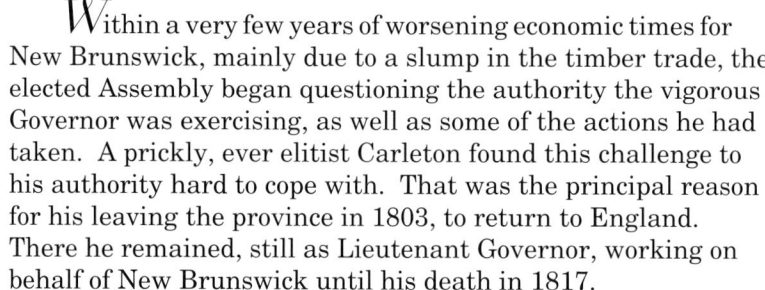

Personal or privy seal of Thomas Carleton, used in his capacity as Captain General and Governor in Chief of New Brunswick. The shield contains the Carleton coat of arms, described by the College of Arms as "ermine on a band sable, three pheons argent." The crest is "on a wreath of the colours argent and sable, a dexter arm embowed habited gules lined argent, holding in the hand an arrow point to the dexter proper."

P.A.N.B.
(P110/509)

Impressive oil on canvas rendering of the Royal Coat of Arms of King George III. It was issued to Governor Carleton for official use in New Brunswick.

P.A.N.B. (P110-507)

Two

A Chivalrous Era

Of the many men of high calibre who have filled the office of Lieutenant Governor of New Brunswick, none served with greater distinction nor made a more significant contribution than did Major General Sir Howard Douglas. Ours was still a young province when in 1824 he took up his post, one to which he brought a rich background of experience as soldier, educator, administrator and writer. His very presence helped create a "chivalrous age" here in New Brunswick, with his viceregal residence becoming the centre of a virtual colonial court.

As soon as he arrived, Douglas turned to improving the living standard of our people. He vigorously pressed for a more dynamic programme of road building, for those he found here were little more than bridle paths. He also showed his appreciation of water communications by having lighthouses built at dangerous points along the coast.

Douglas found time for travel in the province, including official visits. One such was to Moncton, then called The Bend, where the day was sunny and a large number of excited residents greeted him. They were impressed by his handsome coach and matching black horses, and especially by the coachman, who was wearing a black hat and frock coat trimmed with velvet. Accounts refer to the "unconcealed admiration of his [the Governor's] blue uniform with gleaming brass buttons, golden epaulets, and large plumed hat. In the eyes of the pioneers, he was a vision of unequalled splendor: The King's Representative."

At the same time, Douglas worked to improve agriculture, obtaining grants and organizing agricultural societies. While he was in the midst of this activity, a disastrous series of fires struck the province, the worst being that which laid waste a great part of the Miramichi area. Even though Sir Howard's own home in Fredericton — Mansion House — had just been destroyed by fire, he went to the Miramichi to study conditions and lent leadership to the survivors. On his return he supported a public relief fund, secured a grant from the Legislature and was instrumental in obtaining 40,000 pounds

An appealing tale is associated with this oil portrait of Sir Howard Douglas. The painting is to be found in the Webster Collection of Pictorial Canadiana at the New Brunswick Museum. As a young artillery lieutenant, and a bachelor, Douglas was serving at Quebec in the late 1790s. There he met a pretty Canadian girl by whom he had a child. He was transferred back to England, but several years later had this likeness painted and sent to his daughter, Marguarite Douglas. It remained in her family until acquired by Dr. Webster for the museum.

New Brunswick Museum

Privy seal of Major General Sir Howard Douglas, Bt., Lieutenant Governor and Commander in Chief of New Brunswick.
P.A.N.B. (P110/510)

from England. His decisive action in this emergency did much to relieve suffering and won him wide praise. The October 10, 1825, issue of the *New Brunswick Courier* had this to say:

> Much as we admire his bravery as a soldier, his indefatigable endeavors to make himself acquainted with the real state of the province, and his profound political sagacity, we admire still more the distinguished efforts he has made in the cause of suffering humanity.

Of all the achievements during his governorship, perhaps the most significant was the checking of American encroachments on our western boundary in 1827. The dispute arose over lumbering operations on the upper St. John. The firm measures Sir Howard took in organizing the defences of the province and the diplomatic tact he showed in dealing with the American representatives in great part prevented an outbreak of hostilities.

Yet, beyond all these accomplishments, he is probably best remembered here for having founded King's College, the forerunner of today's University of New Brunswick. To do this he first secured a Royal Charter for the modest College of New Brunswick, which had been founded in 1800, and then obtained funds for the erection of the University's Arts Building, an impressive Georgian structure which is still in use.

All the while the remarkable Sir Howard Douglas was dealing with the loss of his home, and the building of its replacement, the lovely structure which still exists as a remarkable landmark. Such was his popularity with New Brunswickers that the Assembly readily agreed to build a replacement, and entirely at the expense of the province. The Governor took a great interest in its design and construction.

The *Royal Gazette* called for designs in its March 14, 1826, issue:

> For a New Government House for the Province of New Brunswick, to be erected at Fredericton, on the site where the Government House formerly stood will be received by either of the following Commissioners, viz:—The Hon. GEORGE SHORE, The Hon. THOMAS BAILLIE, RICHARD SIMONDS, Esquire, or GEO. F. STREET Esq. in Fredericton, or by CHARLES J. PETERS, Esq. in Saint John, until the 13th day of April next.—The Building to be of rough stone, of the Country, laid in courses with hewn quoins and slate Roof. It is requested that specifications may accompany the designs, and those who wish to give in Proposals for Contracts for the whole or any part of the work, must send estimates as well as specifications, to accompany their designs, any approved plan, that will not exceed the sum of £10,000, in the expense of erecting the Building, will be adopted in preference to those of a more extended scale, and premiums will be given for such designs, sent in with specifications and estimates as the Commissioners shall adjudge to be the best and second best.

The winning design was that of Major John Elliott Woolford, Barrack Master at Fredericton, and he was to serve as architect. The call for tenders in the April 22 *Royal Gazette* stated in part:

> Sealed tenders will be received by either of the Subscribers, or by Charles T. Peters, Esq. in Saint John, until Tuesday the 16th of May next, at noon, from such Persons as may be disposed to enter into Contracts for the building of a Government House, for the Province of New Brunswick, on the site of the last one, in the vicinity of Fredericton, according to the adopted Plans and Specifications which are to be seen at the residence of J.E. Woolford, Esq. in Fredericton,

and at the office of C.T. Peters, Esq. in Saint John. Tenders will be received either for the whole work, or for the Stone and Brick work; Carpenter's work, Plastering and Glaising; Painting and cast Iron Balcony, separately, as Persons wishing to Contract may be disposed to undertake.

Actual construction began with the laying of the cornerstone on July 1 by Sir Howard Douglas. That event attracted "persons of all descriptions," according to the July 4, 1826, *Royal Gazette*. The account continues by saying that when the stone—containing a selection of the gold and silver coins of the day—was mortared in place, "His Excellency received from the hands of the Architect in succession the Plumb, the Square and the Level, each of which he applied to the Stone, in their proper positions, and after giving three strokes with the mallet, upon it pronounced it to be 'well formed, true and trusty.'"

The engraved plate accompanying the cornerstone bears the name "J.E.WOOLFORD, Arch't." Woolford was a man of many parts. As well as being Barrack Master and managing the military barracks, he found time to draw and paint, and to design some of Fredericton's most distinguished buildings. In addition to the viceregal residence they include the Arts Building at UNB, the Soldiers Barracks and the York County Jail. The first three have been declared of national significance by the Historic Sites and Monuments Board of Canada. That surely is high tribute to his architectural skills.

Happily, a set of his plans for Old Government House has been preserved at the Public Record Office in London. The PRO kindly provided the Provincial Archives with an excellent photographic copy of the set. Included are plans for the front, river and gable elevations, as well as floor plans.

The classically inspired design for the south facade—the road-front elevation—of the gubernatorial mansion. It was a plain but dignified building, imparting a sense of order and harmony. The centrally located semicircular portico and main doorway give distinction to the residence, as do the bay windows in the pavilions at either end. It was a large building for its time and place, measuring one hundred by forty feet overall.

Public Record Office, London

Old Government House: a pictorial history

The north face, or river-front elevation, as drawn by Major Woolford. To be noted is the veranda or covered balcony stretching the length of the building, at the main floor level. There is a centre bow to this facade, with a stairway leading to the "pleasure grounds" and the river landing below.

Public Record Office, London

The principal public areas, the dining room and the drawing room, were located on the side facing the river. Between them was the breakfast room, which, on social occasions, doubled as a ballroom.

Facing the road were the offices of His Honour, the Executive Council and the aide-de-camp to the governor, together with the waiting room, library and music room.

The upper two storeys were used as the private apartment of the governor. The second or bedroom floor included a state bed chamber, and others for family members, as well as guests. His Honour also had his own dressing room and bathroom. The top floor, resembling a large attic space, was used as staff quarters, and for storage.

There was also a basement in the building, housing the service area, as well as rooms for the butler, the housekeeper and for other service staff, the kitchen and pantry, a dairy and the staff dining hall. Intriguing is the fact that there was a sub-basement, its access door long since sealed over.

Impressive in its style and size for that time, when New Brunswick's population was no more than 150,000, it is seen to be a three-storey building with a gently sloping hip roof and single-storey end pavilions at all four corners. The ably constructed walls were made of locally cut stone, with quoins fashioned from Westmorland County sandstone.

Erected between 1826 and 1828 at a cost of between 10,000 and 15,000 pounds to the province, the viceregal residence was a tribute to Sir Howard Douglas and an indication of the confidence New Brunswickers had in themselves and the likelihood of growth and prosperity. An early visitor, Joseph Bouchette, considered it a handsome dwelling and deserving of the vigor-

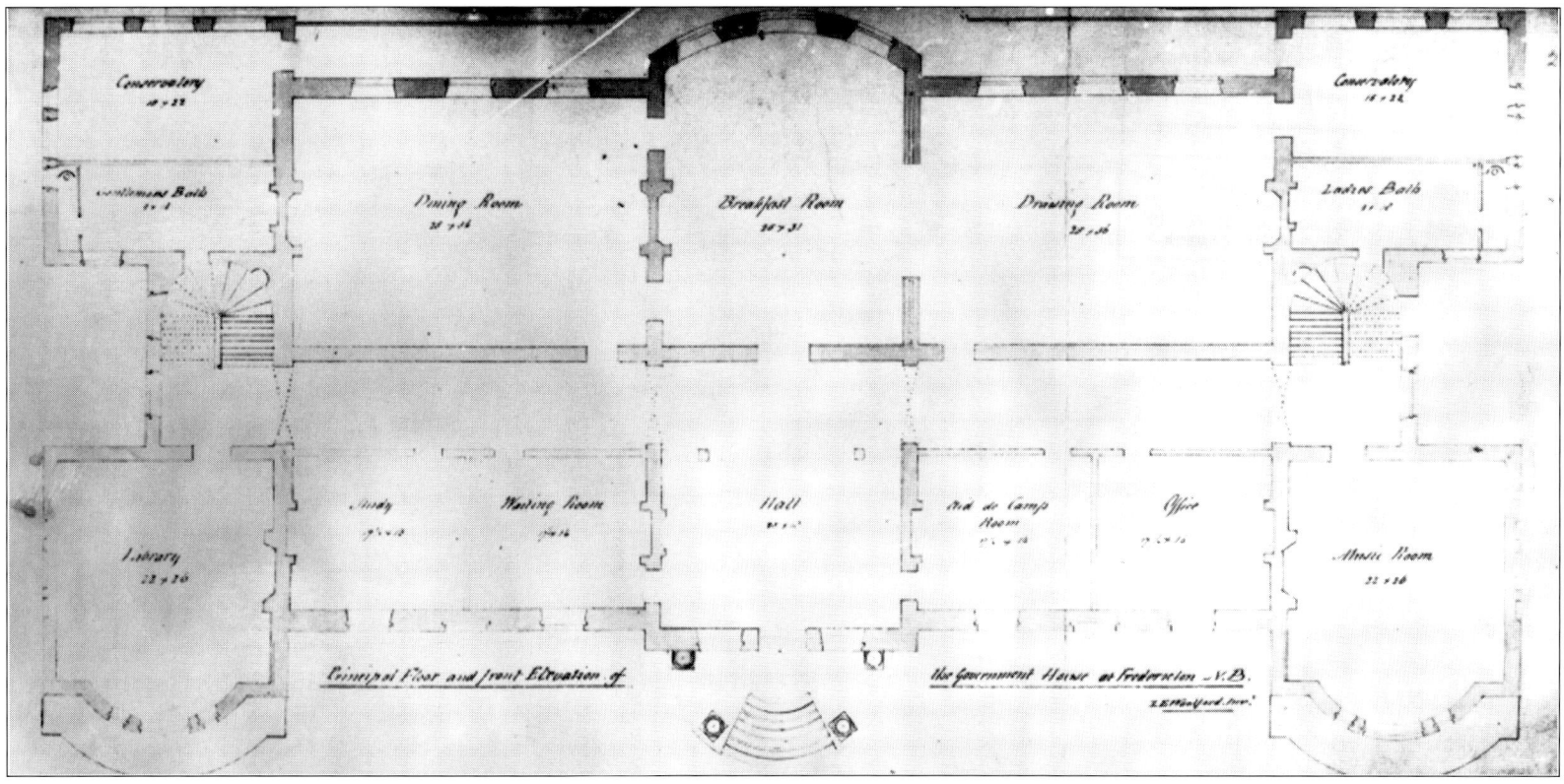

The principal or ground floor plan of Government House as prepared by its architect in 1826. It provided for a generous front door which opens into an imposing and well-proportioned columned entrance hall. This foyer then leads into a central hallway, or "passage" as it was then called, running between staircase halls located at the ends of the building.

Public Record Office, London

---

ous colony. While granting it was a "credible and comfortable building," he felt that the "flourishing province" was capable of "something still more worthy." Other early observers found it "a handsome colonial mansion of stone", "substantial and spacious", and declared it a "testament to the builder's skill and the ability of its architect."

The opening ceremony marking the completion of the building's construction was held on the last day of 1828. Later, the Governor and his First Lady invited a "large Party" to dine with them, and "the evening passed off with conviviality." A "most gratifying and grand festival" put the finishing touch to the opening of Government House. It was a viceregal ball, described as a "highly interesting and joyful event." In an article written for the *Canadian Magazine*, Mary Robinson waxed enthusiastic:

The earliest view we have of the new Government House appeared in Joseph Bouchette's *The British Dominions in North America,* published in 1832. Col. Bouchette, an artist himself, describes it as being "a correct view," the work of "an accomplished young lady," most likely one of the three Douglas daughters.
P.A.N.B. (P4-3-95)

This was among the most brilliant events in the social annals of the province, every colony in King George the fourth's American domains being represented. Lackeys and attendants resplendent in uniforms busied themselves announcing the guests. Militia men patroled the grounds, soldiers in scarlet tunics stood as guards of honor at the gates or attended great personages as aides de camp, while officers of high rank shone in gold braid, chevrons and epaulets or balanced tall shakos crowned with cockades upon their heads, looking very dashing indeed, and honored dignitaries in sombre garments mingled with proud and portly matrons and well known provincial belles more frivolously arrayed.

That premier gala set a tone. Joyful singing, fine concerts, animated dancing, elegant dinners and card parties are just part of the social levity associated with the place during the tenure of Sir Howard and Lady Douglas. While the building's prime function was to provide quarters for His Honour's residence and office, it also became the hub of the colony's social activities.

One of the guests at the opening ball wrote in the *Royal Gazette* about the furnishings:

The three grand rooms are elegantly furnished and were most splendidly lighted. The conservatory had a most pleasing effect and was profusely furnished with rare exotics and surrounded with paintings of rural establishments and rustic scenery. In the midst of this enchanting spot was a most fair tree richly furnished with apples of a golden and most alluring appearance.

A number of the early guests at Government House remarked on its furnishings, which were a harmonized mix of the old and the new, adding to the grace and style of the interior spaces. Thanks in part to the cool-headedness of Lady Douglas, many articles were saved from the burning Mansion House in 1825. They found a place in the new dwelling, as did a quantity of pieces which were ordered for the new structure. The majority of the new items of furniture were supplied by Thomas Nisbet of Saint John, possibly Canada's foremost cabinet-maker of the last century. Happily, a number of those objects from the early years of Old Government House have survived, some now forming the Government House portion of New Brunswick's Provincial Heritage Collection.

A Chivalrous Era

A Regency-style mahogany veneer sofa, impressive for its rail, curved arms and distinctive feet. While said to be the work of Alexander Lawrence, who produced a number of items of furniture for the provincial government, it more likely was made by Charles Humphrey, another Saint John cabinet maker. The sofa is presently in use at the office of the Lieutenant Governor.

New Brunswick Government House Collection

Oil painting of John Holroyd, the first Earl of Sheffield, by M.A. Shee, a member of the Royal Academy.

Speaker of the Legislative Assembly

While it was not there during the opening, this oil portrait had a special association with Government House of the early years. When Governor Sir William MacBean Colebrooke arrived to take up his duties here in 1841, he requested that the Legislative Assembly place a painting of the Earl of Sheffield in Government House, and it was so done. It is also recorded that the portrait, while at Government House, was used for target practice, by the bow and arrow-armed sons of the Governor! Today it can be seen, impressively repaired and restored, in the Council Chamber of the Legislative Assembly Building.

Sheffield was a British privy councillor and an authority on matters of commerce. In New Brunswick, he was viewed as a "kind of patron saint" for his successful efforts to preserve protective sea-borne trade between Britain and our colonial province.

Edward Winslow had commissioned the painting of His Lordship in 1806 on behalf of the grateful Legislative Assembly, for Province Hall, the predecessor of the present Legislative Assembly Building. The impressive sum of 150 guineas was voted for the purchase and delivery of the picture to Fredericton.

The pedestal drum table pictured here was likely the most historic piece of furniture to be found in the new residence. It may have come here with the Loyalists from New York. Around it the Governor's Council gathered and deliberated, first at Mansion House and then in its replacement.

The table's top revolves, and contains twelve pie-shaped drawers. Each of the councillors had his own drawer, together with a vertical compartment in the pedestal base. Today this striking artifact is to be found in the Council Chamber at the Legislative Assembly Building, Fredericton.

New Brunswick Government House Collection

Old Government House: a pictorial history

Lithographic view from a drawing by Edward Thomas Coke, titled *Government House, Fredericton*. It appears in his *A Subaltern's Furlough: Descriptive of Scenes in Various Parts of the United States, Upper and Lower Canada, New Brunswick, and Nova Scotia, During the Summer and Autumn of 1832*. It was published the next year in London.
New Brunswick Legislative Library

The site of the new structure had a history predating the establishment of New Brunswick as a province. It was the location of the 18th-century Acadian village of Sainte Anne, which survived until attacked and burned early in 1759. The Acadians and the Maliseet Indians had long lived at this site in peace and friendship with one another. Their shared cemetery there has been studied, and an archaeological survey has revealed that the land was extensively used over a long period of time by diverse peoples, both Native and European. We know that the grounds once had a church, a priest's house and the Acadian village, which survived the Expulsion by five years. Later that same site was the location of a pre-Loyalist trading post and a variety of late 18th-century houses and other buildings, none of which has survived.

A section of the decorative plaster cornice that was—and still is—to be found in the drawing room.
Author's Collection

Recording his impressions of the new Government House, Coke wrote: "In point of situation and style of architecture it far exceeds both that at Quebec and the one at York and, with the tastefully laid out pleasure-grounds and garden, occupies a large tract of ground on the margin of the water above the town."

He and some of the other early visitors to New Brunswick have provided the best impressions we have of the new residence of the colony's popular Governor. They found it to be "plain but imposing and pleasing in its proportions," in all a "massive, handsome stone mansion, a substantial and spacious one of fine freestone." Another observation was that it was "at once elegant and commodious, with a good lawn and gardens, and pleasant walks along the bank of the river."

A Chivalrous Era

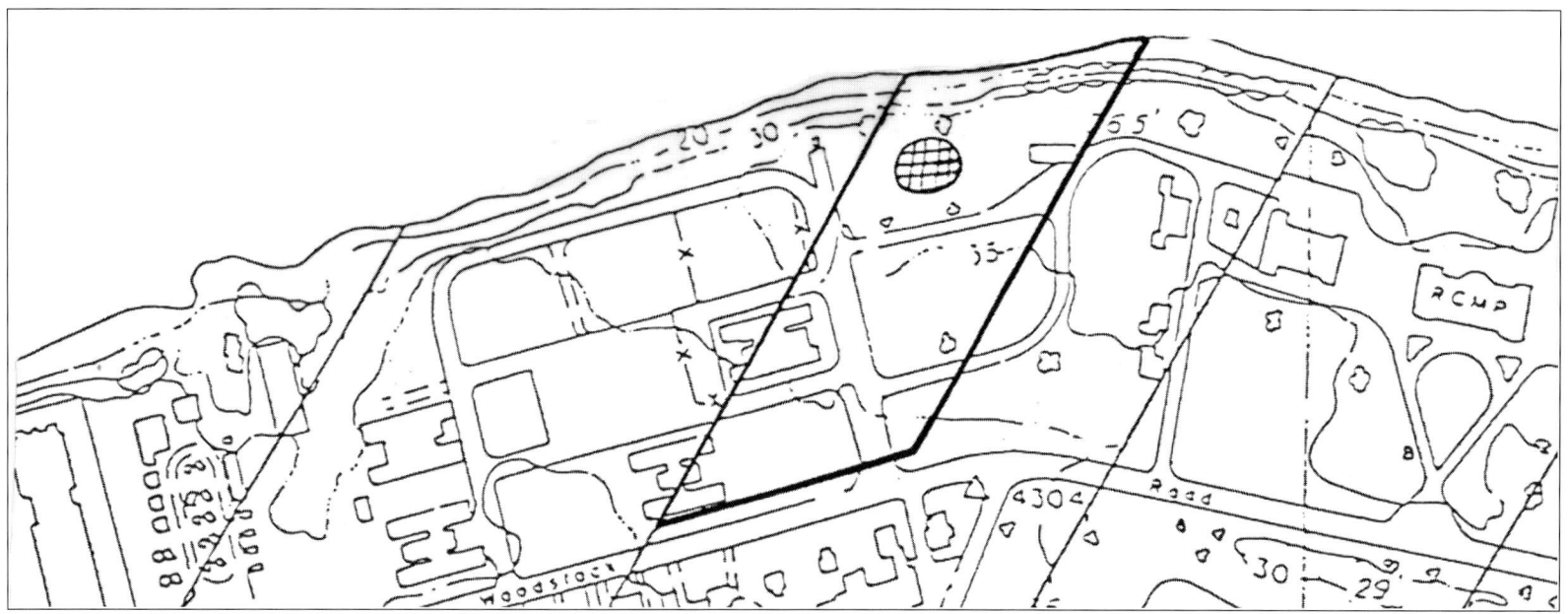

Map of the Old Government House site. Outlined is the portion described in a formal 1768 grant of approximately four acres of land which included "The Indian Burying Ground, House and the Ground on which the Chapel and the Priest's House formerly stood."

Author's Collection

The new Government House could boast of having twenty-three acres of grounds, three of them devoted to a garden and the "pleasure grounds." There was a certain affinity, a blending between the building, its interior and the lovely park-like setting. From the very beginning, the grounds were a striking feature. They extended back in time to Governor Carleton, who had experimented with crops suitable to the new province. As time passed, and the stone presence of Government House became a part of New Brunswick life, croquet lawns, formal grounds, ornamental gardens and a lush growth of shrubs and trees were to make it the showplace of Fredericton.

The Colonial Farmer of Fredericton enthused in its July 18, 1864, issue:

> Standing in this garden on a fine summer morning in the humming silence of the air amidst odors from a hundred flowers, sweeter far than the extract artificial which they call *mille fleurs*, taking in at a glance varied tints of flower, shrub, sward, bush and tree, one feels how beautiful a spot of earth, with care, taste and culture can be made.

The newspaper also reported enthusiastically about the striking variety of flowers that were to be seen growing there, many of them still familiar and popular today. There were German astors, stock, phlox, hollyhocks, dahlias, Japan pinks, and portulaca to form the borders. Elsewhere were to be found scarlet geraniums, verbenas, "splendid carnations," petunias, peonies, roses and herbaceous plants, and fine zinnias. In all, the account makes the gardens sound delightful.

A part of the extensive grounds of Government House is depicted in this wood engraving, from a sketch by Woolford. To be noted especially are the Buttery and the residence beyond, while the river is seen on the left, curving around what was then called Government Point. An illustration contained in Abraham Gesner's *New Brunswick; with notes for Emigrants*.

New Brunswick Legislative Library

The Buttery on the Government House grounds in Fredericton. This undated pencil sketch is attributed to J.E. Woolford.

Royal Ontario Museum

An integral and rewarding part of the grounds was the St. John River with its broad expanse of water and the background of rolling hills. In the heyday of Old Government House the river was a scene of waterborne activity. There were the woodboats and sloops, the lumber rafts and tow boats, the birch bark canoes and Durham boats passing by the viceregal residence and adding to its appeal.

The grounds included several out-buildings. At various times there is reference to a scullery, the wash-house or laundry, to the coach house, stable and sheds, together with the cow house. Then there were the guardhouse, sentry box and, not to be forgotten, a well-house. But surely of all the structures which have stood on the grounds of Old Government House, the most striking is the Buttery. That distinctive circular stone building, erected for use in food storage, likely dates from the Carleton era; we don't know exactly when it was constructed.

As it happened, Sir Howard was able to enjoy the new residence and its grounds for only a short time. He was recalled to England in 1829 to serve as a key advisor regarding the Maine-New Brunswick boundary, then under arbitration, and to press for New Brunswick's best interests in the timber trade. Other work on behalf of British North America also required his talents, although he intended to return to New Brunswick.

However, he felt obliged to resign the lieutenant governorship in 1831. That news was received by New Brunswickers with "heartfelt regret at the loss of their much beloved ruler." Even following his resignation, Governor Douglas continued to work actively on behalf of the province, while pursing a distinguished career as a parliamentarian, colonial administrator, author and inventor.

Surely he was one of the ablest and most popular of New Brunswick's governors, and he received a number of "tokens of esteem" for his contributions to the betterment of the province and her people. For example, when His Honour ceased to be Lieutenant Governor, there was a public subscription and the people of New Brunswick presented him with a handsome silver tea-tray which is now in the collections of the New Brunswick Museum. On it is inscribed:

> "As a memorial of the grateful sense they entertain of the ... persevering zeal and distinguished ability with which he often advocated the Commercial interests of the Province."

Three
A Colonial Social Centre

A "crusty old soldier," Sir Archibald Campbell, succeeded Sir Howard Douglas. The new governor held himself in high esteem, giving a special image to his office. One of his first official acts was to sign the papers authorizing the hanging of a convicted killer. A contemporary news item states that the scaffold was erected on Brunswick Street between Barrack Lane and the entrance to the Loyalist Cemetery.

An amusing story involving the Governor is to be found in W.T. Baird's *Seventy Years of New Brunswick Life*. Actually, it had to do with a Fredericton character named Archy McLean who had served with a Highland regiment. It appears that he and Sir Archibald met and talked from time to time. Now Archy had the habit when his pension money arrived to have several nips, then dress in a Highland kilt and parade about. One day in just such a state he met Governor Campbell, who offered to let him live at Government House if he would care for the cattle there. It was an indignant Archy who shouted, "Na! A McLean will never be a coo boy for a Campbell!"

Social activity at Government House continued to be an important part of the responsibilities of succeeding governors. A social custom quite distinctive in nature was well established at the building by the time of Campbell's occupancy: His Excellency would entertain the Maliseets of the Fredericton vicinity on New Year's Day. They would arrive dressed in tribal costume for the occasion and be received in the elegant Drawing Room. There they mingled with the other guests, and were treated to such things as tea and cakes.

Those others who had also been invited, a "highly respectable assemblage of persons," took an active part in the proceedings. Often to the accompaniment of a military band, they would dance to the music: waltzes, quadrilles, and perhaps even a jig!

In due course the Governor would ask the Chief and other men of the tribe to show some of their dances. A report of one of these annual Government House visits was carried in the *Royal Gazette* of January 1841:

> Friday last being New Year's Day, a large body of the Malecite Tribe of Indians, including a considerable number of well dressed Squaws, and headed by their respected all Chief THOMA, attended at Government House to pay their compliments to the Representative of the Sovereign, and were received by His Excellency with great kindness. The Principal Officers of the Government with their Ladies and Families, including the Junior Branches, and the Officers of the Garrison were present, and the Band of the 36th attended. After their reception, several of the Dances of their Nation were performed by thirty or forty of the Indians and their Squaws in the great Drawing Room; after which a Waltz and Quadrille were danced by several of the young Ladies and Gentlemen present, at the request of the Indians.
>
> His Excellency availed himself of this occasion, publicly to decorate the worthy old Chief with a splendid silver Medallion suspended by a blue Ribbon, exhibiting a beautiful effigy of our gracious Queen on the one side with the Royal Arms on the reverse—one of several similar Badges which we understand His Excellency the Governor General has been liberally pleased to place at the disposal of the Lieutenant Governor.

Old Government House: a Pictorial History

*T*he collections of the McCord Museum in Montreal include a rare interior view of Old Government House. It is a watercolour sketch made by Sir John Campbell entitled *Indian Dance*. The scene depicts the yearly visit of the Maliseets on January 1, 1835. It is a fine piece of documentary art, filled with detail of the "beautiful and spacious" drawing room and its occupants, rendered with remarkable clarity. It reveals details of the handsomely ornamented ceiling from which was suspended a splendid Irish cut-glass chandelier. It was capable of diffusing a brilliant light over the happy scene. At the back of the room are elegant draperies, while a then fashionable Brussels carpet covers the floor.

The artist's caption reads: "A most faithful representation of the Indian Dance at Government House, Fredericton New Brunswick on the 1st of January 1835, at which Major W.N. Grange was present. Drawn by Captain J. Campbell, 38th Regt. A.D.C. to his Father Sir Archibald Campbell, Bart, KCGB. and now Brigadier General."

A strikingly similar watercolour, by the same artist, is to be found in the collections of the York-Sunbury Museum in Fredericton. Unfortunately, it has been badly cropped, but on the back is the artist's signature, matching that in the handwritten caption of the McCord sketch.

York-Sunbury Historical Society Museum

A Colonial Social Centre

Sir John, the son of Sir Archibald Campbell, was an accomplished amateur artist. He did several other New Brunswick sketches, the best known of which is entitled *New Brunswick Fashionables*. This lithograph by J.W. Giles from a drawing by Campbell presents a lively winter scene in Fredericton of 1834. It is noteworthy for its humorous touches as well as the exact treatment of figures and buildings. Governor Campbell's fine sleigh, being drawn by four prancing horses, is seen in the right foreground. Nearby is a group of Maliseets viewing all the goings on with amusement.

Beaverbrook Art Gallery

Time passed, the monarch's representatives came and served their time, then passed from the New Brunswick scene. Each put his individual stamp on the office, in dealing with the challenges to be faced as Lieutenant Governor. Noteworthy is the fact that an impressively large number of them served with distinction.

Government House continued to be the social centre. Sir John Harvey, who lived there from 1837 to 1841, proved a particularly generous host. Records suggest that while the Legislature was in session "he gave three dinners every week, and a ball every fortnight." This gaiety was contagious, and dinners and balls were the order of the day with the prominent citizens as well. "The spacious public rooms served in turn as drawing and reception rooms, banquet hall and ballroom." Sir John found Government House to be of "an admirable size" and "quite spacious enough for every public purpose."

Old Government House: a Pictorial History

*F*urther insights in terms of Government House as a social centre are provided by some of those prominent citizens. An example is to be found in the letters of James Robb, then a professor at King's College. He wrote in 1841 that "The new Governor, Sir William Colebrooke, is an excellent person, infinitely better than the blathering unsteady Sir John Harvey. Sir William and I are very great friends. His Lady and daughters and Secretary are very musical and we and the Costers go up often to make music at Government House."

The *Loyalist and Colonial Advocate* of August 1, 1844, carried this advertisement:

Concert

Mr. Keyzer has the honour to announce to the inhabitants of Frederiction and its vicinity, that he will give a CONCERT on the evening of Thursday, the 1st of August, under the Immediate Patronage of his Excellency, the Lieutenant Governor, and Lady Colebrooke, for which evening His Excellency has kindly allowed the use of the Legislative Council Chamber . . .

Entrance at the Round Tower.

In the social context, Government House served as host to many visitors, some of them rather distinguished individuals. One was the celebrated ornithologist John James Audubon. He was a guest at the viceregal home in 1832 and while there made sketches. Writing in his *Ornithological Biography*, Audubon refers to the print of the pine finch which is found in his *The Birds of America*: "The specimens represented in the plate were procured near the residence of Sir Archibald Campbell, Bart. in New Brunswick, of which Province he is Governor and I have great pleasure in informing you that, through his most polite attention and kind hospitality to myself and family, our time passed in the most pleasant manner while we sojourned in the pretty village of Fredericton."

The "Round Tower" referred to in the concert announcement was undoubtedly the building more often termed the Buttery.

Public Works Canada

Audubon's pine finch, sketched at Fredericton in 1832.

New Brunswick Legislative Library

A Colonial Social Centre

Below: The artist William Henry Bartlett made four trips to Canada between 1836 and 1852. His wash drawings were published in *Canadian Scenery Illustrated* by N.P. Willis, London, 1842, and have proven an invaluable pictorial record. Shown here is an engraving from a sepia sketch by Bartlett made during a visit to Fredericton in 1835.

It is a fine view, from the opposite side of the river. The tranquil scene has a woodboat, canoe and raft in the foreground, while the House itself is admirably made the centre of attention. In all, this rendering illustrates just how beautifully situated was Government House. As *Canadian Scenery* records: "The Governor's House stands a short distance from the town, in one of the most romantic and picturesque situations imaginable. It is a light and elegant structure, forming a very agreeable object from the river, surrounded as it is by ornamental plantations, and sheltered by fine upland slopes, clad with rich and beautiful foliage."

P.A.N.B. (P4-3-96)

Above: This portrait of Audubon was painted by his sons, John, who did the background, and Victor, who drew the figures. A gun was one of the tools of Audubon's trade; throughout his career as a naturalist-artist, he relied on shooting birds for study. Sometimes he ate the birds he shot and offered comments on their palatability.
American Museum of Natural History

Old Government House: a Pictorial History

Another Fredericton view by W. H. Bartlett. The accompanying text reads in part:

> Fredericton, the seat of government of this province, is agreeably situated on a level neck of land, on the south side of the River St. John, about ninety miles above its mouth. The appearance of the town and the adjacent country, viewed from the rising ground behind Fredericton, is highly beautiful and luxuriant . . . the handsome residence of the governor occupies a charming site near the water. . . .
> The best view of Fredericton is had from the opposite side of the river, from whence the town presents a very pleasing appearance.

New Brunswick Legislative Library

A Colonial Social Centre

New Brunswick Government House Collection

The Bartlett sketches appeared soon after Queen Victoria's marriage to Prince Albert. That joyous event was indeed a cause for celebration, and celebration there was! The March 28, 1840, issue of the *Fredericton Sentinel* carried a lengthy account of the rejoicing at the viceregal residence. Here it is in part:

> The Entertainment at Government House in honor of Her Majesty's Marriage, took place on Thursday evening, when the whole of the noble suite of rooms on the ground floor, including both wings were brilliantly lighted and thrown open.
>
> The company began to arrive soon after 9 o'clock, and before 10 nearly 300 guests had assembled, including the Chief Justice, the Speaker, the Members of the Executive and Legislative Council, the House of Assembly, Judges, law Officers of the Crown, Heads and Officers of the Civil and Military Departments of the Province, Lieut. Colonel Maxwell, and the Officers of the 36th Regiment, and of the Garrison of several Officers of the 69th Regiment from the Garrison of St. John, and several gentlemen from that place, with the ladies of their respective families; when dancing commenced in the great drawing room, the Band of the 36th Regiment, under the direction of Mr. Seaume being stationed in the conservatory which had been tastefully arranged and fitted up as an orchestra for the occasion.
>
> The LIEUT. GOVERNOR and Lady HARVEY received their company in the great central drawing room; refreshments were laid in the billiard room, and card tables in that and in the opposite wing; these two rooms being connected by the spacious passage 120 feet long, lighted and furnished with chairs, sofas, etc. which formed a delightful promenade for the company.
>
> The supper tables were laid in the great dining room, of which the doors were thrown open soon after 12 o'clock; when all were struck with the elegance and profusion which the tables presented.
>
> After some time passed in doing justice to the repast, His Excellency in his usual distinct and energetic manner, proposed the toasts. . . .
>
> . . . Never have we witnessed a burst of more enthusiastic feeling than followed each of these short and animated addresses—Indeed His Excellency was frequently interrupted in delivering them by the cheers of his delighted auditors.
>
> After His Excellency and Lady Harvey had retired from the supper room, their healths were proposed and received in a manner to evince the warmth of feeling, justly entertained towards the present inmates of Government House. It is needless to add, that dancing was renewed with, if possible, an increased degree of zest, and the company separated about 3 o'clock with expressions of the highest gratification with the enjoyment of the evening.

Four
Changing Times

From all accounts, the most scholarly of the early colonial governors was Sir Edmund Head. He arrived on the New Brunswick scene in 1848, just as the role of his office was changing. Over the years the power of the Governor had been gradually passing to that of the Legislature. As his biographer has noted in the *Dictionary of Canadian Biography*, Governor Head in the "frontier society" of New Brunswick "still had to be prepared to direct as well as to invite advice, to instill vigour in administration as well as to counsel prudence in the management of resources, and to encourage self-reliance as an antidote to the tendency of blaming all economic evils on the home government."

Governor Head proved to be impressively suited to making the adjustment toward a change from authority exercised by the monarch's representative to that of the elected members of the Legislature. Still, Head was able to write in 1849 that "a Governor's power is mainly that nothing can be done without him." To again quote his biographer:

> The vigour of Head's ideas, the invariable clarity and grace with which he expressed them, his understanding of the physical necessities of government and of those human qualities which make its course run smoothly and swiftly, all added to the stature of his office and to his own claims for affectionate remembrance.

Sir Edmund Walker Head, who served with distinction as Lieutenant Governor of New Brunswick from 1848 to 1854, when he was appointed Governor General. He is credited with implementing "responsible" government while serving as New Brunswick's representative of the Crown. To be noted, too, is that Sir Edmund was an early and able advocate of a federation of the British North American colonies.

From D.G.G. Kerr's Sir Edmund Head, a scholarly governor

Lady Anna Maria Head was the wife of Sir Edmund Head, Bt. Her picture appears in *Types of Canadian Women* where she is described as "a woman of fine presence, bright and intellectual, who did the honours with much tact." In that volume, the editor noted that "she sketched beautifully, and . . . when on a visit to Ottawa, in 1857, she drew a picture of the view from Major's Hill, which she subsequently presented to Queen Victoria, and this, with her Ladyship's vivid description of Ottawa and its surroundings . . . had weight with the Queen, as within a month or two after this event Her Majesty chose Ottawa as the seat of Government of United Canada."

TO

HIS EXCELLENCY

SIR EDMUND HEAD, BART.,

LIEUTENANT-GOVERNOR OF THE PROVINCE OF NEW BRUNSWICK,
&c. &c.

Dear Sir Edmund,

I dedicate these volumes to you, partly because they contain, among other matters, the observations I made during a lengthened Tour through the province of which you are the Governor, and in the prosperity of which you feel so lively an interest. But I do so chiefly as a mode of testifying the respect and regard I entertain for yourself and your family, and as affording me an opportunity of expressing my sense of the many acts of kindness I experienced during a prolonged stay at Fredericton, under your hospitable roof.

Believe me, Dear Sir Edmund, with great respect,

Your obedient Servant,

JAMES F. W. JOHNSTON.

Dedication page from Professor James Finley West Johnston, an agricultural scientist, in his *Notes on North America, agricultural, economical, and social, 1851.*
New Brunswick Legislative Library

New Brunswick Legislative Library

Changing Times

This drawing by Lady Anna Maria Head of the river facade of Government House reveals much by way of detail. A prominent feature of the view is the generous veranda, with conservatories "profusely furnished with rare exotics" at either end leading into the interior of the house. The *Colonial Farmer* of July 18, 1864, argued that "the front of the house is at the back, that is, it looks upon the river, and before it stretching out to the fence on the river's bank, is the ornamental garden and pleasure ground."

P.A.N.B.
(P110-28)

Below: Another appealing drawing by Lady Head. It is Government House as seen from across the St. John River, near the mouth of the Nashwaaksis Stream.

P.A.N.B.
(P110-29)

Lady Head was well thought of here in New Brunswick. Words like "fine presence, bright and intellectual" were used, but it appears that her singing ability left something to be desired! In an 1850 letter to his mother, Professor Robb observed that "Lady Head does not sing very well, but she is fond of Scotch and German music and Judge Carter knowing her taste, has just arranged a pretty Scotch song, a favorite of hers, as a Chorus, with some solos, which she sings herself." Dr. Robb also recorded that the determined Lady organized a Musical Society which met at Government House each week.

Old Government House: a pictorial history

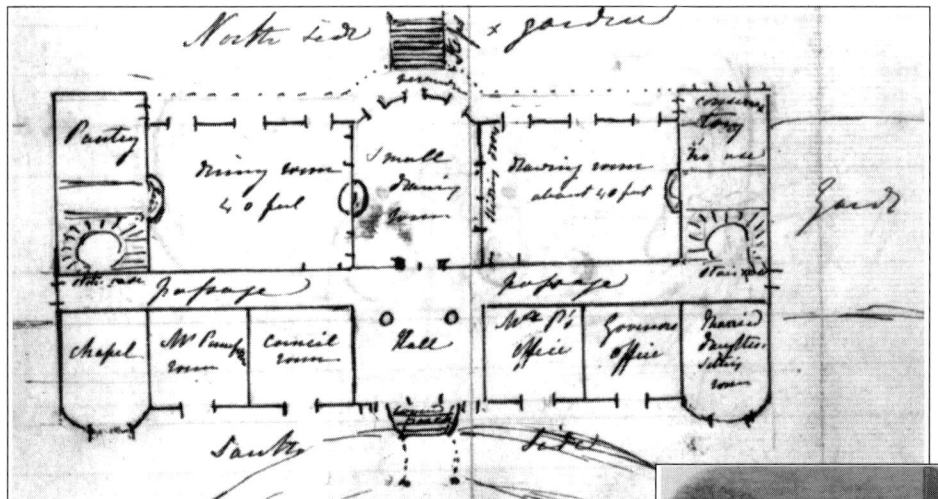

Below: There were many and varied celebrations at Government House over the years. This engraving of a drawing by E.J. Russell of Saint John appeared in the *Illustrated London News* for July 17, 1858. Shown are the firemen of Fredericton, presenting a torchlight demonstration to celebrate Queen Victoria's birthday

Author's Collection

Ground floor plan of about 1850 as sketched by Sir Edmund Head. In this part of the residence, Sir Edmund provided a variety of entertainment. A frequent guest at these events was Professor Robb, who wrote to his mother in 1855: "I was kindly entertained by Sir Edmund Head and repaid him by licking him afterwards at chess."

P.A.N.B.
(P110-26)

Changing Times

The first "kingly personage" to visit New Brunswick's Government House was Albert Edward, the Prince of Wales, who later was to become King Edward VII. As this 1860 *Illustrated London News* engraving shows, a "grand assembly" of people was at the wharf near the end of St. John Street, waiting for the steamer *Forest Queen* to land her royal passenger, and the completion of the still unfinished grandstand!

During the memorable trip upriver from Saint John, the Prince was accompanied by the Lieutenant Governor, Sir J.H.T. Manners-Sutton, and the Legislative Council, as well as members of the House of Assembly. Undoubtedly a good time was had by all. The public accounts record reveals that it was a thirsty enough trip. Some 144 bottles of ale and porter, 12 bottles of pale brandy, 7 of sherry and 21 of champagne were consumed during the voyage.

Author's Collection

Old Government House: a pictorial history

HRH The Prince of Wales, at the age of seventeen, when he visited New Brunswick and resided at Government House.
New Brunswick Legislative Library

𝒫rince Edward landed to be greeted by the firing of Royal Artillery guns, the vociferous cheers of "the assembled crowd," the playing of the 63rd Regiment band and a merry pealing of bells. He then proceeded through two "prettily arranged arches" to Government House, where changes had been made to provide him with a newly furnished and renovated sitting room and bedroom. The short time in Fredericton must indeed have been a busy round of activity for the seventeen-year-old prince. Mention is made of a torchlit march by firemen to Government House, to "a great fire balloon" that rested overhead there before falling into the St. John. It was at Government House too that he held a levee, and also welcomed a group of Maliseets who danced for him on the lawn. That evening he gave a state dinner and hosted a Royal Ball. Also included in the busy but "convivial" visit was a special service at the Cathedral, where the Bishop "delivered a beautiful sermon, one of the grandest sermons ever heard in New Brunswick's capital." Before that service, though, Prince Edward had succeeded in slipping away from Government House and his entourage. They discovered him in a birchbark canoe, being paddled by Gabe Acquin to the Maliseet village on the far shore of the river. Pleas for the Prince to return caused Gabe to paddle back to Government House. Obviously His Highness was impressed by the outing. Before leaving Fredericton he asked to have a Maliseet canoe and carved paddles to take back with him to

Chief or Sachem Gabe Acquin, from a sketch by J.H. Ewing. It is said that the impressed Prince of Wales invited Gabe to visit London. He did go to London in 1883, complete with canoe and wigwam, where he camped at the ponds of South Kensington and became "the greatest social lion of the day."
Wakefield Public Library, England

Changing Times

J.R. Hamilton in his *Our Royal Guests* notes that, referring to his 1860 visit, "King Edward is said to have complimented the house, saying that it was more like a handsomely appointed English residence than any other at which he had been entertained during the tour."

That regal visit was a highlight, probably one not again matched in terms of later regal and viceregal guests at Government House. Yet, collectively, they led Mr. Hamilton to the opinion that, "Among its proud moments are those when it has entertained royalty."

P.A.N.B.
(P4-3-99)

England. After some searching the Royal wish was gratified.

Here in New Brunswick, Sir Edmund had been succeeded by J.H.T. Manners-Sutton, later Viscount Canterbury, as the eighth Lieutenant Governor. From the outset he had differences with the Legislative Assemby, mainly regarding "real" responsible government. One of the topics of disagreement, and a somewhat unusual one, had to do with prohibition. The Legislative Assembly had passed a bill outlawing the importing of alcoholic drink into the province. Convinced as he was that the new law could not be properly enforced, Manners-Sutton took effective measures to force the government's resignation. The resulting election lead to a repealing of the prohibition law.

On the whole, Manners-Sutton enjoyed his years here. Socially, Government House did not suffer during his residency. The first "coming out" party recorded was that of his daughter. By all accounts, that was a merry occasion, highlighted by dancing, when the most popular tune was "Pop Goes the Weasel."

Five

Government House and Confederation

At the very centre of Old Government House's status as a national historic site is the crucial part it played in the bringing into being of Canadian Confederation. Of the many important roles that the building played in the life of New Brunswick, none equalled the place it had as the site of major political decision making. Many were the storms of government debate which swirled about the building during its years as the viceregal residence. Yet none matched the struggle associated with the bitter disagreement and pivotal events that determined New Brunswick's path to Confederation.

Central to the taking of that rough and turbulent path was Sir Arthur Hamilton Gordon, New Brunswick's Lieutenant Governor during those early years of the 1860s leading to Confederation. Gordon had arrived in the province in 1861, to take up his first appointment as a colonial administrator. Many terms have been used to describe the complicated and controversial Gordon. Writings about him contain such descriptions as "aristocratic," "arrogant," "full of assurance," "intelligent," "honest," "egotistical," "humorless and unbending." He was to be judged in time as "one of the outstanding British colonial governors" of his period of public service.

Sir Arthur Gordon, circa 1870.
From J.K. Chapman's The Career of Arthur Hamilton Gordon, First Lord Stanmore

Government House and Confederation

Gordon's first three years here were peaceful, and he came to love this country. Still a young and healthy man, he was a great outdoorsman who travelled to every corner of the province. The Lieutenant Governor wrote in his book *Wilderness Journeys in New Brunswick*:

> Few things are more delightful than to drop down some great river, where a very frequent turn presents, notwithstanding the monotony of continual forest, some new view; and where, as you smoothly glide on, a perpetual succession of fresh pictures is presented to the eye.... After some days spent in salmon fishing, partridge shooting, etc. we again started, and leaving my companions to follow me more leisurely, I proceeded to the Pabineau Falls, below which I was to find a carriage to take me to Bathurst. Quitting the canoe in a rapid above the falls, I walked alone across the bare granite rocks which separated me from the party waiting my arrival, and which also formed the dividing line between the wilderness and civilized life.

In Gordon's time Government House even had a collection of live birds and animals, native to the province, assembled by the Governor himself during his outings in the "bush."

Regarding the Confederation issue, the instructions Sir Arthur received read: "you will . . . express the strong and

The Governor became good friends with George T. Taylor, a pioneer photographer of the out-of-doors who by times accompanied Sir Arthur on his wilderness travels in the province.

P.A.N.B.

Carved on the top of the lid of this wooden box are the words "His Excellency Hon. A.H. Gordon, Fredericton No. 3 New Brunswick." It is believed to have been used to contain supplies during the Governor's wilderness travels. It could also be pressed into service as a makeshift table or even a seat. This was a Governor who loved the out-of-doors.

New Brunswick Government House Collection

Old Government House: a pictorial history

Arthur Hamilton Gordon and his party on one of his wilderness trips. The photograph was taken by George T. Taylor, probably on the banks of the Tobique. The Governor is seen standing toward the front of the group, which includes the noted Indian guide Gabe Acquin.

P.A.N.B.
(P42-64)

George T. Taylor of Fredericton, a friend of Sir Arthur Gordon, had taken his first picture — a daguerrotype — by 1856. Soon after he adopted the new wet-plate process. Taylor became well known for his work as a pioneer outdoor photographer. The results are indeed remarkable. An impressive collection of his work has survived and is to be found as a part of the Beaverbrook Photographic Collection at the Provincial Archives. (X821)

Chief Acquin frequently guided Governor Gordon on his wilderness journeys, and a friendship developed. He was a natural leader and is credited with the founding of the St. Mary's Indian Reserve, diagonally opposite Old Government House, in Fredericton.

From F.D.H. Vieth's Recollections of the Crimean Campaign

Government House and Confederation

deliberate opinion of Her Majesty's Government that . . . all the British North American Colonies should agree to unite in one Government."

Gordon had come to believe in such a course of action. In practical terms, a federation of the provinces would not be possible without New Brunswick since it was located between the Canadas and Nova Scotia. In the New Brunswick he had come to care for he had watched while each section of the province, jealous of the others, had put its own local needs ahead of the needs of the province as a whole. He had seen their politicians fail to work together, and too often act unwisely. One big, central government would stop all that, or so he thought.

Back in those years of the mid-1860s, most New Brunswickers saw little to be gained from a federation of the British North American colonies. An election was fought over the issue and the anti-Confederation party led by Albert J. Smith was successful. The pressure on Gordon to "do something" about the situation mounted. As the Queen's representative he was able to exert considerable influence, and within the governing circle did so. He gauged that the Smith government was far from united on the Confederation issue. Government House and its master became a "centre of operations," its aim, one filled with frustration, intrigues and persuasion, was to bring about the Canadian union. Governor Gordon did not hesitate to woo uncertain members of the Legislature, and he won some of them to the support of the Confederation forces. It was at Government House in 1866 that, as the Historic Sites and Monuments Board plaque states, "occurred the historic encounter between Governor Arthur Gordon and Premier Albert J. Smith which precipitated the fall of the anti-Confederation government and prepared the way for the union of the Provinces."

New Brunswick's delegates to the 1864 Charlottetown Conference aboard the steamer *Anna Augusta* as she prepares to leave Fredericton. Sir Arthur Gordon is said to have done a great deal to bring about the conference. It was to lead to Confederation in 1867.

P.A.N.B. (P5-146)

In this photograph by George T. Taylor, Governor Gordon and his support staff are seen at the portico of Government House. His Excellency is the figure standing in the doorway.

P.A.N.B. (P5-897)

Old Government House: a pictorial history

Government House as seen from Woodstock Road. The photograph was probably taken during Sir Arthur Hamilton Gordon's term there as Lieutenant Governor. Writing of the building in *Arts of New Brunswick*, architect W.W. Alward describes it as "an imposing stone structure of Georgian design. It is a quiet and dignified composition with a central carved portico of the Doric order, balanced at both ends of the front elevation, by low projecting wings having some circular bays of pleasing proportions." He also admired its classically inspired architecture and excellence of design, referring to it as an architectural landmark.

National Archives of Canada
(P5-856)

Government House and Confederation

A watercolour sketch by J.H. Ewing showing Lieutenant Governor Colonel Francis Pym Harding's sleigh during a ride he had organized on January 20, 1868. Government House is to be seen in the right background.

Harding had received his viceregal appointment in the fall of 1867, Confederation year. He was to serve until a native-born governor could be agreed upon.

Wakefield District Library, England

The Governor had given a great many parties in his time. He had entertained big wigs and little wigs, the passing military and the local grandees. Everybody who had the remotest claim to attention had been attended to: the ladies had had their full share of balls and pleasure parties: only one class of the population had any complaint to prefer against his hospitality; but the class was a large one — it was the children. However, he was a bachelor, and knew next to nothing about little boys and girls: let us pity rather than blame him. At last he took to himself a wife; and among the many advantages of this important step was a due recognition of the claims of these young citizens.

This quotation is from J.H. Ewing's *Canada Home*. Mrs. Ewing, a writer of stories for children and a talented artist, was a frequent guest of Lieutenant Governor Harding at Government House during his term of office from October 18, 1867, to July 23, 1868.

Six

From Rebirth to Twilight Years

Confederation needed both good politicians and first-rate businessmen. Operating such a central government would be a large undertaking, and one that would spend considerable amounts of money. New Brunswick's Samuel Leonard Tilley was admirably suited, and quickly became a key figure in Canada's first federal government.

Tilley had been born in Gagetown, an appealing town beside the St. John, and in a house which today is home to the Queen's County Museum. There he lived the first thirteen years of his life, where his grandfather had come as a Loyalist settler in 1783. Like so many upriver boys, young Tilley moved down to the city of Saint John, seeking his fortune at the early age of thirteen. There he found work as a druggist's apprentice and by the age of twenty he was joint owner of his own pharmacy, a business that was to grow and prosper. Tilley also made time for community activities, such as the Saint John Debating Society. As a talented and popular public speaker, it seemed only natural that he would find his way into politics. There he was impressively successful. Elected to the Legislative Assembly in 1850 he proved to be a strong presence, striving always for better government. He fought for progress: a better system of government, improved education, railway lines and, most of all, a union of the British North American provinces. In that cause, as head of his party, he travelled to all corners of the province, vigorously expounding the benefits of Confederation.

In the march toward a federal union, Tilley, with wit and sagacity, played a leading role at the conferences in Charlottetown, Quebec and again in London. With the achieving of Confederation through the British North America Act in 1867, Tilley described the new Canada as "a Dominion stretching from sea to sea," and Queen Victoria accepted the term, naming the new nation the Dominion of Canada.

Samuel Leonard Tilley was an effective and influential member of Canada's first federal cabinet under Sir John A. Macdonald. When the Macdonald government resigned late in 1873, Tilley, at the age of fifty-five, was appointed Lieutenant Governor of New Brunswick. It was a popular appointment. From the outset he demonstrated acumen, cordiality and an ability to "reach people, to inspire." His sincerity and honesty of opinion were evident to all. Sir Leonard stands out in his capacity as New Brunswick's Lieutenant Governor, truly filling the office with a high degree of effectiveness.

Sir Samuel Leonard Tilley, 1818-1896. This leading Father of Confederation was probably serving his second term as Lieutenant Governor when this photographic likeness was taken.

P.A.N.B.
(P5-198)

From Rebirth to Twilight Years

A fine bust of Lieutenant Governor Sir Samuel Leonard Tilley by John Rogerson, a Saint John wood carver who achieved fame for his work. He was especially outstanding as a sculptor of figureheads to grace the bows of sailing vessels of the time.

Sir Leonard is seen wearing his knighthood insignia, conferred by Queen Victoria in 1879 in recognition of his effective work for Confederation.

New Brunswick Museum

An engraving of Government House from the *Canadian Illustrated News* of 1872, a year before Leonard Tilley's appointment as Lieutenant Governor. It was sketched from about the corner of Smythe Street and the Woodstock Road. The cows provide a wonderfully pastoral touch. To be noted as well is the castellated gateway leading to the entrance at the eastern end of the House.

P.A.N.B. (P4-3-98)

In speaking of the popular Governor, who was an ardent supporter of the Temperance Movement, the *Reporter* carried the comments of a visitor to Government House, a Mr. White of the *Montreal Gazette*, in 1874:

> . . . never was a Government House so popular, and never was a Governor so completely the idol of the whole people. If Mr. Tilley does not give wine at Gov't House he entertains in other ways most lavishly, croquet parties in summer, dancing in winter are the means among others he adopted to show that wine is not an inevitable necessity of enjoyment. And Government House, under his presidency and that of Mrs. Tilley, who is emphatically and in the best sense of the word his helpmate, is not the exclusive property of officialdom, but is open to the people generally. Mr. Tilley has done much for his native province in the past; but I may be permitted to doubt whether he had done a greater service to them in showing that firm adherence to professed principles . . .

Old Government House: a pictorial history

Writing about Fredericton's Government House-centred social life of that time in *The Story of Fredericton*, Marjorie Thompson quotes the words of the distinguished educator Sir George R. Parkin recalling life in the capital in the 1870s and 1880s:

> Indeed, in all my wanderings since then I have seldom formed social surroundings and intellectual influences more helpful and inspiring. My wife and I often speak of the immense advantage we gained from living in such surroundings as we had in the Fredericton of our early days. There was an old-fashioned courtesy and dignity — a real interest in things of the mind and spirit, which seem to have somewhat disappeared in the rush of life and supposed progress of later times.

As "admirable" chatelaine of Government House, Alice Starr Tilley displayed organizational skills, good humour and a lively interest in social activity. The *New Brunswick Reporter* happily stated in 1874 that "The Lieut. Governor and Mrs. Tilley have won golden opinions by their generous and courteous demeanor on the occasion of the first Ball at Government House. The affair passed off with decided eclat, and was highly enjoyed by a large and brilliant assemblage." And taking note of a second ball to be held soon after, the newspaper enthused that "It will be a most brilliant affair, unrivaled in its attractions, and unsurpassed by any similar occasion in the celestial city."

Over a long and active life Lady Tilley, as she became when her husband was knighted in 1879, was an impressive helpmate to Sir Leonard. Her zeal, general knowledge, common sense and individuality were demonstrated during her years at Government House. An aspect of these qualities is illustrated by an observer at a winter outing at the Soldiers Barracks in 1885.

> Sir Leonard himself drove over to these festivities to present the target practice prizes. The Governor's sleigh has a pretty pair of bays. Lady Tilley has introduced tobogganing with a slide on the grounds and opened it Christmas Day. The sport was grand. There is a commodious waiting room at the top, an easy stairs up one side and a dragway for toboggans up the other. The chutes are 150 feet long, sloping one foot in three and a half they say, so descent is rapid and carries them well out onto the river ice.

This able Lady was a leading member of the National Council of Women. She became widely known for her benevolent work, and was prominent in the establishment of several hospitals in the province. To be noted is her presidency of the Red Cross in New Brunswick during the First World War. Political historian Arthur Doyle refers to her affectionately as

Lady Tilley, looking quite regal in appearance as she posed for this studio portrait. It probably dates from the late 1880s.

P.A.N.B. (P5-202)

From Rebirth to Twilight Years

Lady Tilley and her husband, seated in a sleigh in front of the main entrance to Government House. Perhaps they were about to leave for the nearby toboggan slide. Incidentally, the photograph reveals a good deal by way of the building's portico and the principal doorway.

New Brunswick Museum

A particularly appealing Taylor photograph of Government House of the 1880s. It is filled with interesting details. Wilmot Park, which the Prince of Wales had opened in 1860, is still in its younger years, judging by the size of the trees around the bandstand. The wooden building with gingerbread trim, seen toward the centre of the picture, was possibly later moved from the Government House grounds.

Old Government House with Wilmot Park and the general streetscape set the character for a sizeable neighbourhood in Fredericton's west end. It is treed, yet open and spacious in an area of remarkable historical character, made all the more so by the presence of the river.

Typical of the Palladian architectural style, the vice-regal residence had two main entrances. The riverside entrance led from a large, manicured "pleasure ground," with a tree and flower garden, and the water's edge. The Woodstock Road entrance faces Wilmot Park, as this photograph shows. Taken together, they represent a significant landmark.

P.A.N.B. (P5-279)

Old Government House: a pictorial history

A photograph of the Governor and Lady Tilley seated in a barouche in front of Government House.

The picture was donated to the museum in 1940. The accession records include a note from the donor, which reads in part: "The site of old Government House is a beautiful spot and certainly added dignity to the Governor's 'job'. As long as we have to have a Governor we should see that he lives right."

New Brunswick Museum

Old Government House, with its conservatory in the right-hand portion of this photograph by George T. Taylor. The framed and glazed greenhouse had been added to the downriver end of Old Government House in 1874. It was judged to be "the largest and most elaborate" in New Brunswick. Accounts of the time tell of "floral beauties," its "rare and choice plants and exotics," and an 1876 newspaper story makes mention of "its beautiful proportions," of the cordial welcome to that "fairy like place" by "our model Lieutenant Governor and his most estimable lady."

P.A.N.B.
(P5-166)

From Rebirth to Twilight Years

Two of Lieutenant Governor Tilley's sons, L.P.D. and Herbert, are here shown in this view from the late 1870s of the still flourishing Conservatory. L.P.D. Tilley grew up to become a politician in his own right and to serve as premier of the province.

P.A.N.B. (P5-41)

A striking picture of the Government House conservatory interior, taken about 1880. Partially obscured by the foliage is a figure, likely that of the gardener.

The conservatory was destroyed early in the winter of 1894, when the roof and side walls buckled under the weight of a heavy snowfall.

P.A.N.B. (P5-215)

Old Government House: a pictorial history

Another — and excellent — photographic view of Government House and its striking conservatory.
P.A.N.B. (P5-163)

"the grand old lady of the New Brunswick establishment."

Governor Tilley actually served two separate terms. Part way through the second, in 1890, he announced his decision not to continue to use his own private resources to maintain Government House, the provincial grant being inadequate. Tilley preferred to live in his own Saint John home and not strain his own purse with the official residence. However, he did reside at Government House when the Legislature was in session and it was necessary for him to be in Fredericton.

By the time he completed his second term in 1893, it was evident that he had proven to be a most able New Brunswick-born Lieutenant Governor. Tilley was an outstanding individual, and he had devoted himself to a better future for the province and its people. He filled the gubernatorial office with a special presence, in all a gentleman leader who shines forth from the pages of our history! On his deathbed in 1896 during an election, he was told that his Liberal-Conservative party was leading in the province. Above all a politician to the end, his last words were, so it is said: "I can go to sleep now, New Brunswick has done well."

Seven

Neglect, Closing and Thereafter

In a private letter written in 1885, R.D. Wilmot expressed his regret that the Legislature was showing so little consideration to "maintaining the position of the Lieutenant Governor with suitable dignity." The previous year, as part of a resolve to reduce government expenditures, a bill had been passed stating that all provincial government funding for Government House operations was to cease, except for those amounts "absolutely required to keep such building and premises connected therewith in necessary repair." No longer would the Province bear the costs of fuel, lighting and furnishings, nor the wages of servants and caretakers. In fact, the reduction in Government House expenditures was gradual, but by 1895 was down to $200 annually. In his 1885 letter Lieutenant Governor Wilmot stated his belief that the Legislature's drastic action "was principally caused by the extravagant expenditure during the 1879 visit of the Marquis of Lorne and Princess Louise when for three or four days the expenditure was about $16,000." In fairness, the records show most of that amount was spent on refurbishing the residence to make it suitable for occupancy by such distinguished visitors.

Certainly the Premier, A.G. Blair, considered Government House to be an unnecessary expense, especially at a time of financial difficulties for the province. In 1893 Government House officially ceased to be the viceregal residence. From then on, and for many years after, the private residences of the successive lieutenant governors were considered to be the government house during their tenure of office. More than one was woefully unsuited to serve that role.

Many awkward situations occurred as a result of this inadequate arrangement. For example, a *Daily Gleaner* headline in 1912 read: "Frogmore to be Government House for Duke's visit. Randolph Estate Offers Place to Lieut. Governor [whose home was in Sackville] to Entertain Royalty." Worth mentioning too is that for a time the residence of the Hon. L.A. Wilmot was leased by the province for the use of the Lieutenant Governor during the annual session of the Legislature. On another occasion, when the Governor-General, Lord Aberdeen, visited Fredericton, he and his suite were grateful to the Misses Fisher for the use of "Summerville" house as their residence.

Most likely this building, with its distinctive ornamental barge boards, once stood on the Government House grounds. Today it is close by, located in Wilmot Park, at the corner of Odell Avenue and Saunders Street.

Old Government House: a pictorial history

Isaac Erb photograph of the building taken at about the time of its closing. The hedges and other plantings give an attractive touch to a truly great structure.

P.A.N.B. (P5-310)

A further step in the demise of Old Government House as the official residence was a two-day public auction during which the entire contents of the building were disposed of, everything from cases of stuffed birds to a water closet. An order in council authorizing the sale had been passed in 1892, and an inventory of the building's furnishings prepared three years later. The *Daily Gleaner* made the auction event headline news: "Members of Government and M.P.P.'s Among the Buyers." "Large Crowds, Lively Interest, Sharp Competition, Good Prices." In its reporting, it described "the drawing room which was completely filled by the eager and attentive throng of purchasers and on-lookers," and "The rooms were crowded almost to suffocation." An ironic touch was added by the purchase of lengths of Brussels carpet, "which the Government bid in for the Lunatic Asylum"! There were 697 itemized articles listed in the printed catalogue which noted that in addition "there will be sold a great variety of miscellaneous goods such as old kitchen utensils, stoves, chairs, books, etc., that could not be very well catalogued." When the sale was all over, the amount realized from the relics proved to be less than $2,000.

Despite vigorous opposition, both political and popular, Premier Blair stood fast, and Government House was not reopened for the use of the Lieutenant Governor. An item in the August 7, 1897, issue of *The Capital*, a monthly newspaper, read in part:

> The Bazaar at Government House on last Dominion day gave thousands of people an opportunity for the first time to inspect the interior of this historic building. A person familiar with Rideau Hall, the Governor-General's residence, at Ottawa, as well as the Government Houses in all the Provinces of Canada, informed us some years ago that Government House, this city, surpassed all of them. Though deserted for years, and ruins of its beautiful conservatory carried away, the expenditure of a few thousand dollars would restore it to its former well-cared state.

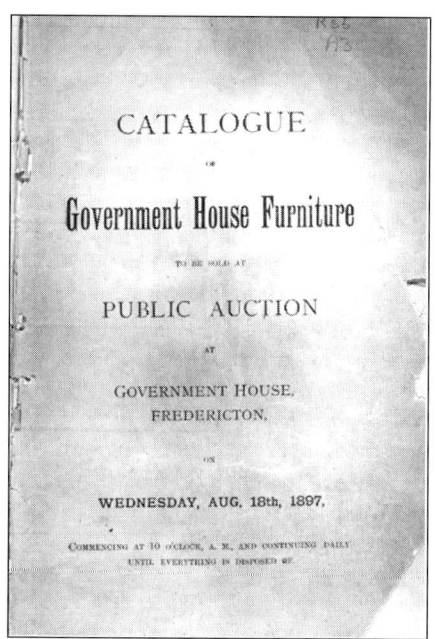

P.A.N.B. (P110-515)

Neglect, Closing and Thereafter

This elegant mahogany banqueting table once graced the dining room at Government House. It is the work of Thomas Nisbet of Saint John, and probably dates from the mid-1830s. The table was puchased at the 1897 auction by G.F. Hill of St. Stephen, then a member of the Legislative Assembly. *New Brunswick Government House Collection*

Imposing wardrobe or press, fitted for hanging clothes. Both its design and craftsmanship are impressive, and reveal that it was made about 1860, the date of the famous visit of the Prince of Wales.

This is a piece with Government House markings. Family tradition has it that it was purchased at the 1897 auction by Mrs. W.G. Clark whose husband was to serve as Lieutenant Governor from 1940 to 1945.

New Brunswick Government House Collection

Labelled walnut hall table purchased for Government House from Hutchings and Burnham, a Saint John firm, in 1860. On the underside of the top is "J.A.E. Co.," the mark of the Boston marble supplier. The table's frame also carries the mark "Gt. House N.B. Hall."

New Brunswick Government House Collection

Elaborately carved mahogany sofa. It is said to have been purchased at the auction of Government House relics. The maker's label of Thomas Nisbet is attached to the frame. Thomas Nisbet was the foremost cabinetmaker of the time in British North America. Many items were produced by this craftsman for Government House.

The accomplished Nisbet had been commissioned in the mid-1820s by Sir Howard Douglas to produce a number of articles of furniture for the viceregal residence. Quite possibly this sofa was one of them.

Private Collection

A strikingly similar sofa, attributed to Thomas Nisbet, is to be found in the collections of the Royal Ontario Museum.

Neglect, Closing and Thereafter

Brass fireplace fender with Government House markings. It is stencilled "G't House N. Brunswick 1861 A.D." and was purchased at the 1897 auction by F.I. Morrison.

For close to thirty years the Provincial Government has been reacquiring Government House artifacts which were auctioned off in 1897. The retrieved items — being held in trust — now number well over one hundred, and they represent an invaluable core in terms of once more appropriately furnishing Old Government House.

New Brunswick Government House Collection

Rosewood card table crafted by Thomas Nisbet. It dates from about the time of the building of Old Government House and is said to have been acquired at the 1897 sale.

Private Collection

Gothic butternut side chair, with hinged seat, ca. 1860. Marked on the underside is "Gt. H. N. B." It is one of a set of "six wooden hall chairs" listed in the 1895 inventory. For many years this piece was used at the Legislative Library.

New Brunswick Government House Collection

Old Government House: a pictorial history

So now the building stood denuded and vacant. Four years later, though, Old Government House became home to the Deaf and Dumb Institute, its own school structure having burned. Then in 1903, the provincial government once more closed the structure. During those sad years following the closing, there continued to be attempts to have the structure restored as Government House, notably by the IODE and the Local Council of Women. In an able article written on behalf of that objective entitled "The Old Government House," which appeared in *The Canadian Magazine* in 1906, Mary Robinson makes a statement which is equally apt today:

> The beautiful Government House which I have described is standing empty, but is in a state of sound repair and of wonderfully good preservation . . . walls, doors, windows, woodwork, foundation — all firm and solid. . . . Do you wonder that the people of New Brunswick are trying to restore to their Province this grand old home of the past as the most suitable and desirable residence that could be provided for . . . her Lieutenant-Governor? In beauty of situation, in architectural design, in dignity of line and feature, this grand old mansion stands unsurpassed by any in Canada.

Despite such efforts, it remained vacant: "Only a caretaker and the ghosts of a more elegant and less practical day walked through its chambers," to quote the *Daily Gleaner*.

In 1916 the property was occupied by the Department of Militia and Defence for use in training the 236th Battalion for trench warfare and for service overseas. As the First World War was drawing to a close, the Department of Soldiers' Civil Re-Establishment used the building as a temporary military

Old Government House had undergone only minor alterations throughout its history, until 1918. At that time, extensive changes were made to adapt it for use as a military hospital. The most striking change in the building's appearance was the addition of the dormers, to provide greater headroom on the third floor. The distinctive veranda, which ran the length of the building on the river side, had badly rotted and was removed at the same time. During its period of vacancy, Government House had lost its conservatory, outbuildings and fences. Only one of the original outbuildings has survived: a small, perfectly round and roofed structure of stone, variously described as the Buttery, the well-house or the smoke-house.

P.A.N.B.
(322B/12)

Neglect, Closing and Thereafter

Despite its sale to Ottawa in 1921, Old Government House was to remain unoccupied until 1934, when the Royal Canadian Mounted Police moved in. The force was to be there until 1988, when a new and larger facility became available.

National Archives of Canada
(PA 49803)

hospital and recuperation centre for returning wounded soldiers. In doing so, fifteen of the third-storey windows, front and back, were enlarged and roof dormers added. It was probably at the same time that the large French doors which opened onto the riverside veranda were replaced by fixed windows, and the veranda itself removed.

In 1921 the Legislative Assembly passed an act which authorized the sale of the building and a portion of the Government House grounds to the federal government, for $50,000. That amount was to be placed in a trust account and used to provide New Brunswick's lieutenant governors with accommodations while in office, including help in defraying the cost of using a private residence for viceregal house purposes.

Thus the building passed from provincial hands, some time later — in 1934 — to become Royal Canadian Mounted Police Headquarters for "J" Division.

Postscript

Happily, Old Government House is available to once again serve as the Lieutenant Governor's residence and office. New Brunswick is fortunate to have a building of the stature of that noble edifice; its proposed use could do much to ensure its giving pleasure and meaning once more as our gubernatorial mansion.

For many years both Ottawa and the province have expressed an interest in having Old Government House become once again the official residence of New Brunswick's Lieutenant Governor. Presently Her Honour occupies a small, inadequate home a short distance downriver, which was meant only as a temporary dwelling for the viceregal couple. Now there is the opportunity to restore Old Government House to the purpose for which it was designed: to be the home and office of the Lieutenant Governor.

Above: Edgecombe House, 736 King Street. Its ground floor presently serves as the office of the Lieutenant Governor. Of special interest is the fact that when Government House burned down in 1825, this building was rented for two hundred pounds a year to serve as Sir Howard Douglas's residence while the new stone replacement was being erected.
New Brunswick Photographic Services

Left: Somerville House, located at 239 Waterloo Row, was adapted and furnished for temporary use as Government House and the official residence of the Lieutenant Governor in 1974. It was built in the 1820s and may have been designed by J.E. Woolford. However it has undergone extensive modifications over the years since.
New Brunswick Photographic Services

Postscript

An exciting adjunct to this possibility is the opportunity to focus meaningful attention on a crossroads of New Brunswick heritage. The property is an extraordinary historical and archaeological resource and a monument to the enduring peoples of New Brunswick. The land on which Old Government House stands has a known history which pre-dates the official establishment of New Brunswick as a province. It is the location of the 18th-century Acadian village of Sainte-Anne, which survived until burned by a force of New England rangers early in 1759. The Acadians and the Indians lived in peace and friendship with one another. Their shared cemetery there has undergone some study. Archaeological surveys indicate the land has been extensively used over a long period of time, by New Brunswick's cultural groups, both early and late. We know that the grounds held a church, a priest's house and the Acadian village which survived the Expulsion by five years. There was a pre-Loyalist trading-post there as well, and a variety of late 18th-century houses and other buildings, none of which has survived.

In turn, Old Government House itself is an absolute gem, one of the jewels of 19th-century Canadian architecture, and it has been designated by the Historic Sites and Monuments Board of Canada as a structure of national significance, both historically and architecturally. With the restoration of the Lieutenant Governor to Old Government House, the property should be enhanced as befits the residence of such a distinguished New Brunswicker.

The Royal Coat of Arms, which was affixed to the portico at the entrance way to the new Government House.
Author's Collection

A detail of the decorative plasterwork, likely dating from the building's construction in the late 1820s. It is a central ceiling medallion, still capable of imparting a feeling of the grand days of Old Government House.
Author's Collection

The building, together with its extensive grounds, could be the setting for a range of state functions and hospitality. It may serve once more as an impartial meeting place, with its official state rooms on the main floor furnished in keeping with its status as the viceregal abode. It is to be expected that certain areas would be open to the public for visiting on a restricted basis, but only with the consent of the Lieutenant Governor. Such visitor access would help instill a knowledge of the history and institutions of the province.

Old Government House: a pictorial history

The viceregal residence is a provincial responsibility, in terms of furnishings as well as the building fabric itself. In this way, New Brunswick entitles her Lieutenant Governor to accommodations appropriate to the high ranking accorded that office, as she did in times past. This is especially true of the official public rooms, where state functions are held and distinguished guests received. Most of all, a renewed and meaningful role would be found for a highly important building.

Professor W.S. MacNutt, speaking at Old Government House in 1962, made a statement well worth repeating:

One of the truly notable things that today gives us reason for meditation is that the province was able, at a time when its population was less than 150,000, to raise and sustain this magnificent residence for the popular Lieutenant-governor, Sir Howard Douglas. The revenues that paid for it were entirely provincial in origin.

Now, 166 years later, New Brunswickers have the opportunity to return this heritage building to its former lively grandeur and its prominent place in the province's profile. That act would also preserve and enhance a particularly rich location in terms of New Brunswick's history. An asset of both provincial and national proportions would result. Surely we are up to the challenge of achieving that long desired goal.

Old Government House is one of the finest late Regency buildings to be found anywhere in Canada. It is widely seen as a national treasure, and it was judged by the distinguished architectural historian Dr. Robert Hubbard to be "one of the greatest houses in the land." This stately mansion has been declared of national significance, architecturally and historically. It awaits a bright future.

P.A.N.B. (322B/13)

Appendix

The story of the governors of the territory we today call New Brunswick stretches back in time to the year 1604. It was then that our first governor, the Sieur de Monts, erected his government house on the tiny island of St. Croix, which has been declared an historic site of international significance. Successive governors followed — French, British, and Dutch as well — with the passing of time. Studying the subject of our governors can prove to be a fascinating attraction. That segment of our past contains a great deal of history, yet it has received scant attention.

Little information is readily available about the importance these governors have had in New Brunswick's growth and development. Here we have a rich store of distinguished individuals important to our history and, through them, links to so many events that shaped and fashioned our area as a distinctive part of Canada.

Today, the province's representative of the Crown is the Lieutenant Governor. This has been the case since 1786, when the title of Governor was changed to Lieutenant Governor. From 1603, customarily it has been governors who were commissioned to be the senior representatives of royal authority over the territory which now comprises New Brunswick.

The task of developing a list of the governors and lieutenant governors of Acadia and New Brunswick carries with it some regret and embarrassment: so little is known of our Indian period, prior to the coming of European settlement in 1603. Our two tribes, the Micmacs and the Maliseets, had lived here for generations. While theirs was viewed by the newcomers as a primitive way of life, still they were here, and with their own form of government. What is more, they represented over 10,000 years of human occupancy, and no list of governors, however official, should entirely overlook that fact.

The record for the early years is not always a straightforward one. Ours was a land which was fought over as countries, notably England and France, vied for supremacy in this portion of the New World. Also, there were times when the conflicting claims of right to govern were not simply between countries but between individuals whose allegiance was to the same monarch. In some cases the available records are not sufficient to make entirely clear who precisely held the office of governor at a given time. Another point of some confusion is the fact that, on occasion, more than one individual shared the governorship of the northern half of Acadia. D'Aulnay and La Tour are examples, as are Crowne and Temple.

In that early period, too, some appointments as governor were by royal commission. But for a number, the source and terms of the appointment to govern is less clear. Again, one might question the right of a particular individual to appoint another to command in Acadia. For example, Poutrincourt's passing his office of governor to his son, Biencourt, or the Marquise de Guercheville assigning her right to govern to Sieur de la Saussaye. Because of the limitations of the available records, and situations such as those described, it was decided that the pre-1784 list should contain the names of those who are known to have exercised the authority of governor. In other words, the right to govern could not always be clearly established. In such cases the listing has been left blank. Hopefully, additional documentation will appear, enabling improvements to the list herein presented.

The distinguished historian and scholar, Dr. W.F. Ganong, in a paper delivered to the Royal Society of Canada in 1895, noted some of these difficulties. He referred to the period before 1760 as being singular and outlined the struggles for control. In fact, he pointed out in his remarks that the pre-New Brunswick territory changed hands no fewer than ten times between 1604 and 1784.

The situation following 1784 is much more straightforward, with each incumbent having been duly commissioned. However, no official list of our New Brunswick governors existed until 1985. At that time, and based on the appropriate research data, the Clerk of the Executive Council certified a list of governors who have served since 1784 with their dates of being sworn into office and terminating that office, and the proper form for names and titles.

For the period prior to 1784, and stretching back to the de Monts settlement on the Isle Ste. Croix in 1604, several lists were available. They provide useful information and represent extensive research: Lejeune, Monet and Hubbard are names that come readily to mind. The *Dictionary of Canadian Biography* was found to be a particularly valuable source of reliable data. Additional study, from a New Brunswick perspective, adds to that information and has been utilized in producing the list which follows.

The period 1710-1760 is an interesting consideration in this context. Most authorities show the governors of Nova Scotia exercising jurisdiction over New Brunswick during those fifty years. In fact, the French refused to recognize any English claim to Acadie north of the Bay of Fundy. Some historians refer to that territory as "French Acadia." It is a matter of record that the land known today as New Brunswick was administered from 1710 to 1759/60 by the Governor of New France. During that time, too, the European settlements here were exclusively Acadian. For those two reasons, the roll which has been prepared for that time span shows the succession of governors of New France during the 1710-1760 period.

So it is that the following catalogue contains the names of those who were governors and lieutenant governors of Acadie and New Brunswick. The dates shown are those for the assuming and the relinquishing of office. Sometimes, usually when the office of governor was vacant, an administrator was appointed. However, the authority of administrators was limited, so they have not been included.

GOVERNORS & LIEUTENANT GOVERNORS
of
ACADIA & NEW BRUNSWICK

Pierre du Gua de Monts
1603-1606

Jean de Poutrincourt
1606-1614

Charles de Biencourt
1614-1623

Charles de La Tour
1631-1642

Isaac de Razilly
1632-1635

Charles de Menou d'Aulnay
1638-1650

Charles de La Tour
1653-1657

Emmanuel LeBorgne
1657-1667

William Crowne
1662-1667

Sir Thomas Temple
1662-1670

Appendix

Alexandre LeBorgne de Belle-Isle
1667-1670

Hector d'Andigne de Grandfontaine
1670-1673

Jacques de Chambly
1673-1677

Cornelis van Steenwijck
1676-1678

Francois-Marie Perrot
1684-1687

Louis-Alexandre Des Friches
1687-1690

Joseph Robinau de Villebon
1691-1700

Jacques-Francois de Bouillan
1701-1705

Daniel d'Auger de Subercase
1706-1710

Le marquis de Vaudreuil
1710-1725

Le marquis de Beauharnois
1726-1747

Le marquis de La Galissonniere
1747-1749

Le marquis de La Jonquiere
1749-1752

Le marquis Duquesne
1752-1755

Le marquis de Vaudreuil-Cavagnal
1755-1760

Charles Lawrence
1760

Jonathan Belcher
1761-1763

Mantague Wilmot
1763-1766

Michael Francklin
1766

William Campbell
1766-1773

Francis Legge
1773-1782

John Parr
1782-1784

THE PROVINCE OF NEW BRUNSWICK

King George III, founder of the Province of New Brunswick 18th June, 1784 and His Successors, together with a further list of their Personal Representatives within the said Province since its foundation. The Governors and the Lieutenant Governors thereof:

Thomas Carleton
1784-1817

George Stracey Smyth
1817-1823

Sir Howard Douglas, Bt.
1824-1831

Sir Archibald Campbell, Bt.
1831-1837

Sir John Harvey
1837-1841

Sir William MacBean George Colebrooke
1841-1848

Old Government House: a pictorial history

Government House, official residence of New Brunswick's lieutenant governors from 1828 until 1890. It continues to be a captivating historic structure. Standing as it does in somewhat solitary splendour, the building conveys a rather haunting sense of past grandeur. Together with its grounds and superb riverside location, Old Government House imparts a strong sense of history and of continuity.

P.A.N.B. (322B/9)

Sir Edmund Walker Head, Bt.
1848-1854

Sir John Henry Thomas Manners-Sutton
1854-1861

Arthur Hamilton Gordon
1861-1866

Charles Hastings Doyle
1867

Francis Pym Harding
1867-1868

With Confederation came a change in the appointment of the Lieutenant Governor. No longer would it be an imperial decision, but one made by the new Dominion and its leader. There was also an understanding that from then on the Lieutenant Governor would be New Brunswick-born.

Lemuel Allan Wilmot
1868-1873

Samuel Leonard Tilley
1873-1878

Appendix

Edward Barron Chandler
1878-1880

Robert Duncan Wilmot
1880-1885

Sir Samuel Leonard Tilley
1885-1893

John Boyd
1893

John James Fraser
1893-1896

Abner Reid McClelan
1896-1902

Jabez Bunting Snowball
1902-1907

Lemuel John Tweedie
1907-1912

Josiah Wood
1912-1917

Gilbert White Ganong
1917

William Pugsley
1917-1923

William Frederic Todd
1923-1928

Hugh Havelock McLean
1928-1935

Murray MacLaren
1935-1940

William George Clark
1940-1945

David Laurence MacLaren
1945-1958

Joseph Leonard O'Brien
1958-1965

John Babbitt McNair
1965-1968

Wallace Samuel Bird
1968-1971

Hedard Joseph Robichaud
1971-1981

George Francis Gillman Stanley
1982-1987

Gilbert Finn
1987-1994

Margaret Norrie McCain
1994-

References

BOOKS

Alexander, Sir J.E. *L'Acadie, or Seven Years Explorations in British America.* London, Colburn, 1849.

Bailey, A.G., ed. *The Robb Letters.* Fredericton, Acadiensis Press, 1983.

Baird, W.T. *Seventy Years of New Brunswick Life.* Saint John, G.E. Day, 1890.

Blom, M.H. and Blom, T.E. *Canada Home: Juliana Horatia Ewing's Fredericton Letters, 1867-1869.* Vancouver, University of British Columbia Press, 1983.

Campbell, P. *Travel in the Interior, Inhabited Parts of British North America in the Years 1791 and 1792.* Toronto, Champlain Society, 1937.

Chapman, J.K. *The Career of Arthur Hamilton Gordon, First Lord Stanmore, 1829 - 1912.* Toronto, University of Toronto Press, 1964.

Clark, N. *Palladian Style in Canadian Architecture.* Ottawa, Parks Canada, 1984.

Coke, E.T. *A Subaltern's Furlough.* London, Saunders and Otley, 1833.

Douglas, Sir H. *Considerations of the Value and Importance of the British North American Provinces.* London, J. Murray, 1831.

Foss, C.H. *Cabinetmakers of the Eastern Seaboard.* Toronto, 1977.

Gesner, A. *New Brunswick, with Notes for Emigrants.* London, Simmonds and Ward, 1847.

Gordon, A.H. *Wilderness Journeys in New Brunswick.* Saint John, 1864.

Hamilton, J.R. *Our Royal Guests.* Boston, Beal Press, 1902.

Hannay, J. *History of New Brunswick.* Saint John, J.A. Bowes, 1909.

Hubbard, R.H. *Ample Mansions, The Viceregal Residences of the Canadian Provinces.* Ottawa, University of Ottawa Press, 1989.

Hunter, A. and Bell E., eds. *The Journal of Sir Martin Hunter.* Edinburgh, 1894.

Johnston, J.F.W. *Notes on North America, Agricultural, Economical and Social.* Edinburgh, W. Blackwood and Sons, 1851.

Kerr, D.G.G. *Sir Edmund Head, a Scholarly Governor.* Toronto University of Toronto Press, 1954.

Larracy, E.W. *The first hundred; a story of the first 100 years of Moncton's existance, etc.* Moncton, Moncton Publishing Co., 1970.

Lawrence, J.W. *Footprints or Incidents in the Early History of New Brunswick.* Saint John, J. and A. MacMillan, 1883.

MacNutt, W.S. *New Brunswick, a History: 1784 -1867.* Toronto, Macmillan of Canada, 1963.

McGregor, John. *British America.* Edinburgh, 1832.

Maxwell, L.M.B. *An Outline of the History of Central New Brunswick.* Fredericton, York-Sunbury Historical Society, 1937.

Monet, Jacques. *The Canadian Crown.* Toronto/Vancouver, Clark, Irwin, 1979.

Peck, Mary. *The Bitter with the Sweet.* Tantallon, N.S., Four East Publications, 1983.

Squires, W.A. *History of Fredericton.* Fredericton, City of Fredericton, 1980.

Swan, Conrad. *Canada: Symbols of Sovereignty.* Toronto, University of Toronto Press, 1977.

Vieth, F.H.D. *Recollections of the Crimean Campaign, etc.* Montreal, Lovell and Son, 1907.

Willis, N.P. *Canadian Scenery Illustrated.* London, J.S. Virtue, 1838-42.

ARTICLES

Bailey, A.G., "Keystone of the Arch," *The Atlantic Advocate*, April, 1964.

Bidlake, G.G., "The Old Government House of New Brunswick," *Family Herald*, October 28, 1925.

Buckner, P.,
- "Sir William MacBean George Colebrooke," *Dictionary of Canadian Biography, Vol. IX*, Toronto, University of Toronto Press, 1976.
- "Sir Archibald Campbell," *Dictionary of Canadian Biography*, Vol. VII, Toronto, University of Toronto Press, 1988.
- "Sir John Harvey," *Dictionary of Canadian Biography*, Vol. VIII, Toronto, University of Toronto Press, 1985.

Gibson, J.A., Sir Edmund Walker Head," *Dictionary of Canadian Biography*, Vol. IX, Toronto, University of Toronto Press, 1976.

Godfrey, W.G., "Thomas Carleton," *Dictionary of Canadian Biography*, Vol. V, Toronto, University of Toronto Press, 1983.

Jarvis, W.M., ed. "Royal Commission and Instructions to Governor Thomas Carleton," *Collections of the New Brunswick Historical Society*, 6, 1905.

Maxwell, L.M., "The Royal Tour of 1860," *Maritime Advocate and Busy East*, July 1947.

McDonald, R.H., "Sir Charles Hastings Doyle," *Dictionary of Canadian Biography*, Vol. XI, Toronto, University of Toronto Press, 1982.

Robinson, M., "The Old Government House, Fredericton, N.B.," *Canadian Magazine*, October, 1906.

Spray, W.A., "Robert Duncan Wilmot," *Dictionary of Canadian Biography*, Vol. XII, Toronto, University of Toronto Press, 1990.

References

Taylor, H.A., "Francis Pym Harding," *Dictionary of Canadian Biography*, Vol. X, Toronto, University of Toronto Press, 1972.

Thompson, M.J., "Domestic Life," in Frank Baird, ed., *Fredericton's 100 Years, Then and Now*, Fredericton, 1948.

Wallace, C.M.,
- "Lemuel Allan Wilmot," *Dictionary of Canadian Biography*, Vol. X, Toronto, University of Toronto Press, 1972.
- "Sir Samuel Leonard Tilley," *Dictionary of Canadian Biography*, Vol. XII, Toronto, University of Toronto Press, 1990.

Wilbur, R., "John Henry Thomas Manners-Sutton," *Dictionary of Canadian Biography*, Vol. X, Toronto, University of Toronto Press, 1972.

Young, D.M., "Sir Howard Douglas," *Dictionary of Canadian Biography*, Vol. IX, Toronto, University of Toronto Press, 1976.

"Monument of Great Historic Significance says Professor," *Daily Gleaner*, Fredericton, June 5, 1962.

About the Author

Dr. MacBeath is a son of New Brunswick, having been born in Moncton and raised in Saint John. He came to admire Old Government House and all that it stood for while a student at the University of New Brunswick in Fredericton.

The author began his work in the heritage field as History Curator with the New Brunswick Museum in Saint John. While there he began his contribution to learned journals, notably the scholarly introductory work for Volume I of the Dictionary of Canadian Biography. After serving as the first Director of the Ontario Science Centre, Dr. MacBeath returned to New Brunswick to become the province's first Deputy Minister of the Historical Resources Administration. Later he served as a member of Canada's Historic Sites and Monuments Board, continuing to concern himself with our New Brunswick Heritage on a national level. Those concerns included Old Government House and its welfare.

While doing his research, George MacBeath found that surprisingly little had been written about Old Government House, despite its being one of the most important landmarks in the St. John Valley, and possibly the most valuable of the historic structures to be found in New Brunswick.

New Brunswick's Old Government House: a pictorial history represents the results of many years of experience and observation; most of all it demonstrates insightful knowledge and devotion to a truly outstanding building.

The author, a Member of the Order of Canada for his contributions to the nation, is now retired and living in Fredericton. There, he continues to demonstrate a lively interest in matters of heritage.